◁▷ALTERNATIVES is a new series under the general editorship of Eric S. Rabkin, Martin H. Greenberg, and Joseph D. Olander which has been established to serve the growing critical audience of science fiction, fantastic fiction, and speculative fiction.

BRIDGES TO SCIENCE FICTION

Edited by

George E. Slusser
George R. Guffey
and
Mark Rose

Southern Illinois University Press
Carbondale and Edwardsville

Feffer & Simons, Inc.
London and Amsterdam

Library of Congress Cataloging in Publication Data

Eaton Conference on Science Fiction and Fantasy
  Literature, 1st, University of California,
  Riverside, 1979.
  Bridges to science fiction.

  (Alternatives)
  Essays prepared for the First Eaton Conference on Science Fiction and Fantasy
Literature, held Feb. 24-25, 1979, at the University of California, Riverside.
  Bibliography: p.
  Includes index.
  1. Science fiction—Congresses. I. Slusser,
George Edgar. II. Guffey, George Robert.
III. Rose, Mark. IV. Title.
PN3448.S45E2 1979   809'.3876   80-16622
ISBN 0-8093-0961-0

Contents

Preface

Critical discussion of science fiction has become fairly sophisticated in the past decade or so; nevertheless, even today, there is some tendency on the part of critics and teachers as well as readers to discuss science fiction as if it were a wholly independent phenomenon unconnected with the mainstream of our cultural inheritance. One purpose of the present volume is to suggest connections between science fiction and other aspects of Western Culture. Ranging in interest from the specifically philosophical to the specifically literary, the essays deal with science fiction in relation to such topics as medieval cosmological discourse, classical empirical philosophy, contemporary philosophy of science, fairy tale, epic, and gothic fiction. A second purpose of the volume is to make a coherent statement about science fiction as a literary form, and the essays are arranged to emphasize the overall logic that emerges from the development of the individual discussions.

The volume begins with Harry Levin's "Science and Fiction," which explores the long history of literary response to science and places science fiction in a wide historical perspective. Whereas "Science and Fiction" deals with the whole field of Western literary culture and thus provides a general background for the other essays, Kent T. Kraft's "Incorporating Divinity: Platonic Science Fiction in the Middle Ages" suggests the connection between science fiction and a single early philosophical school. The next two essays continue the concern with philosophy, but move into more modern and perhaps more familiar areas: Stephen W. Potts suggests how Stanislaw Lem can be understood as dealing with the epistemological issues raised by Locke, Hume, and Kierkegaard; Gregory Benford further develops the epistemological question of the knowability of the truly alien and considers this subject in the light of contemporary philosophy of science. Kraft, Potts, and Benford have been concerned with ways in which science fiction is involved in areas that overlap the traditional concerns of religion. Robert Hunt focuses on this region of overlapping concern in his discussion of the portrayal of religious revelation in science fiction.

With Eric S. Rabkin's "Fairy Tales and Science Fiction," the volume moves from the consideration of specifically literary matters. Patrick Parrinder considers science fiction in relation to epic, and Thomas H. Keeling reexamines the proposition that science fiction developed from the gothic novel of the late eighteenth century. Next, Carl D. Malmgren studies the way in which science-fictional worlds distinguish themselves from other narrative worlds. Finally, in a theoretical statement about the genre as a whole, Thomas A. Hanzo suggests a point of view from which many of the questions implicit in the earlier essays can be answered, a point of view from which further discussion of science fiction might begin.

Nine of the authors in this volume are literary scholars; one is a physicist and science fiction writer. Some are well known; some are appearing here for the first time in print. Some have previously written a great deal on science fiction; some are presenting their initial statements about the genre. From this diversity, however, we believe that there emerges both a coherent view of science fiction as an important literary form and a sense of its complex relation to our cultural heritage.

The essays in this volume are all original and were all written specifically for the first Eaton Conference on Science Fiction and Fantasy Literature held February 24–25, 1979, at the University of California, Riverside. The Eaton Conference, centered in the University Library's Eaton Collection of Science Fiction and Fantasy Literature, one of the finest in the world, is an annual gathering of international scholars and writers devoted to discussion of problems concerning these literatures and, on a broader plane, science and fantasy in modern art and culture in general.

The editors would like to thank Eleanor Montague, University Librarian, University of California, Riverside, and Jean-Pierre Barricelli, Chairman of the Department of Literatures and Languages, University of California, Riverside, for their untiring interest in science fiction and the Eaton Conference. Without their support neither the conference nor the essays presented here would have come to be.

George E. Slusser
George R. Guffey
Mark Rose

Riverside, California
March, 1980

Bridges to Science Fiction

Science and Fiction

Harry Levin

Since my three-word title echoes those two nouns which denote the subject of this symposium, it should be self-evident that my own key-word is the conjunction between them. Not that I would wish to put asunder what has clearly been compounded with so much imagination, industry, and ingenuity. The copula is merely my confession that I have little right to expatiate on the compound. Though I have had frequent opportunity to read and write and talk about various forms of fiction, my encounters with the genre that we have been invited to discuss—enjoyable and instructive as they may have been—have been somewhat casual and slight. As for science, I can only confide that in my case the ordinary layman's interest has been enhanced, if not solidified, by a number of happy associations with professional scientists through academies, common rooms, and personal circumstances. Yet I realize, as I begin to fill in the pages that follow, that I am adopting the simple-minded tactic of the journalist in *Pickwick Papers*. Having been assigned an article on Chinese Metaphysics, it will be remembered, he looked up both China and Metaphysics in the encyclopedia and thereupon combined the information. As a bug-eyed alien among a galaxy of experts, I feel something of the thrill that must alert the interplanetary voyager. Since the rhythms of my thought are conventionally measured by academic semesters rather than light-years, we may have some degree of mental synchronization to work out among us. Such considerations do not make the adventure less exciting for me; but, not wanting to travel under false colors, it should be clear from the very outset that I view myself as rather a tourist or passenger than a pilot or guide.

3

Perhaps we may take our chronological bearings by noticing that we now stand within five years of 1984. Reading the newspapers, we may even wish to congratulate ourselves on having come so near to fulfilling George Orwell's projections for intercommunication and cognition: Newspeak and Doublethink. Orwell made his prognostication in 1949, thereby allowing us another lustrum for its fulfillment. One decade afterward, just exactly twenty years ago, C. P. Snow delivered his reverberating pronouncement on *The Two Cultures*. This, as the problematic formulation of an important issue, has weathered better than F. R. Leavis's virulent counterattack. There has meanwhile been some tendency, I suspect, for scientific and literary sensibilities to come closer together. What could be a better witness to that than science-fiction? Can there be a scholar-teacher or writer-critic here who could not respond correctly to Snow's elementary shibboleth for scientific literacy: the Second Law of Thermodynamics? On the other hand, there must be some who put forth, or lend credence to, fictive postulates that have still to be acknowledged by Snow or Carnot or the canons of physics itself. One of my colleagues who was awarded a Nobel Prize in that field, and who reads extensively beyond it, has testified that Snow's early novel *The Search* is the only book that conveys what it feels like to be a practicing scientist today. Other scientists have written fiction, Kepler in elaborately phantasmagorical form. Still others, even closer to the Cavendish Laboratory than Lord Snow, have written autobiographical accounts of what has been going on there. But, though James Watson's *Double Helix* chronicles the discovery of DNA, his underlying themes are human competition and vanity.

Literature, taken in its broadest sense, has acted as an agent for the dissemination of science. Some of the most technical treatises, in the early days, were couched in poetic modes. The Greeks and Romans read Aratus and Lucretius for information about meteors and atoms. Indeed the evocation of Epicurus, at the beginning of *De Rerum Naturae*, "proceeding far beyond the flaming walls of the firmament," is a more eloquent tribute than any Nobel Prize winner has ever been paid. Dante, in transit through the celestial regions, listens to a lecture from Beatrice on gravity. Chaucer is transported to his House of Fame by an eagle who discourses upon the principles of acoustics. Scientific popularizers, like Fontenelle and Algarotti, wrote as if they were novelists addressing themselves to feminine readers. The scientist himself, when cast as a literary character, has played an equivocal role: a subspecies of the archetypal trickster, a man of many inventions like the elusive Odysseus, a fabulous artificer like Daedalus, who became Joyce's archetype for the artist. Faust was the prototype of the modern mage, though it was never wholly clear whether he had dedicated himself to a disinterested quest for wisdom or to an egoistic cult of experience. His case is shadowed by a primitive taboo against forbidden knowledge, like the parable of Frankenstein—or, for that matter, Adam or Prometheus. Unlike Faust's demonology, Prospero's white magic—what Shakespeare called his "art"—could be entertained as proto-science, a command over nature through an understanding of its inherent properties and hidden interrelations. This was, to be sure, the original purview of alchemy, from which we can trace surviving concepts of chemistry and physics, not to mention Jungian psychology. Yet its consistent failure to live up to its gilt-edged promises made it for several writers—Chaucer, Erasmus, Ben Jonson—a hoax to be exposed. For Balzac it was a characteristic obsession: *La Recherche de l'absolu.*

Since the techniques and objectives of empirical research are likely to seem arcane and hieratic to the uninitiated, these have become a target of philistine satire, to be caricatured by Aristophanes with his sophistical think-tank or by Swift in Gulliver's *reductio ad absurdum* of the Royal Society. The contraptions of the late Rube Goldberg, where unlikely concatenations of home-made machinery are circuitously arranged to bring about what might otherwise have been accomplished by a simple human gesture, may be viewed as a critique of our increasing dependence on push-button gadgetry. The clysters and phlebotomies and embrocations and faddish operations and bedside manners of physicians have made them popular butts on the comic stage from Molière to Shaw. Yet the worldly success of such charlatanism was grounded upon a quasi-religious awe, as Molière himself intimated: an acceptance of quacks as a priesthood conniving, for better or worse, in the powers of life and death. With contrasting reverence, Balzac apotheosized the doctor as humanitarian benefactor in his *Médecin de campagne;* and, though the husbands of Emma Bovary and Carol Kennicott were mediocre rural practitioners, they were men of bumbling good will; while Sinclair Lewis, with the cooperation of the bacteriologist Paul De Kruif, surveyed the heights and depths of the American medical establishment in his *Arrowsmith.* The physician, after all, is often the only person of scientific training that most other people ever get to see very much. When, instead of going on his clinical rounds, he isolates himself within a laboratory, his experimentation gets clouded in mystery, and he is perceived as a sinister figure, coldly or madly treating humans as guinea-pigs: Dr. Rappacini, Dr. Heidegger, Dr. Jekyll, Dr. Moreau.

Historically, we are well aware that the line of demarcation between science and pseudo-science is difficult to draw, not less so because accepted theories are continually being confuted and discarded. Rationalists have attempted to sharpen it by their satirical exposures. But we also know that science-fiction battens on pseudo-science: that alchemy, astrology, phrenology, mesmerism, and ESP adapt themselves much more aptly to fictitious narration than do the more quantifiable disciplines. Thus Brian Aldiss cites the inspiration of Gurdjieff and Ouspensky, whom he terms "the slav dreamers"—he might likewise have mentioned Velikovsky. Precisely because of their illusory assumptions, such mystagogues and gurus are more at ease in the realm of illusion than, let us say, Planck, Rutherford, or the Joliot-Curies would be. This distinction may help to explain why Milton, though he was fairly well abreast of contemporary astronomy, chose to locate the scenes for *Paradise Lost* in a Ptolemaic rather than a Copernican universe. Even so, he dared allude to Galileo's telescope, the "optic glass" of "the Tuscan artist," and he must have felt something of that tension between Christian dogma and the new cosmology which would be ironically dramatized by Brecht in his *Galileo*. Hamlet, in his brief metaphysical poem addressed to Ophelia, had made no secret of his own heliocentric skepticism: "Doubt that the sun doth move." The gradual consequence of such anti-geocentric reductionism was to shatter those chains of being which had related man, in his central position, to the correspondent influences of the zodiac and the universal harmony of the spheres—to relocate his earth as a lesser outpost in a plurality of worlds. A second and even more shattering reduction was to come, as we shall be noting, with Darwin. But it was already enough of a shock to raise the question, which would pulsate back and forth from *King Lear* through Thomas Hardy, of nature's indifference to mankind.

The sense of chilling detachment and emotional deprivation, as it bore upon the novelist, might be brought home by this paragraph closing a chapter from an early story of George Eliot's:

> While this poor little heart was bruised with a weight too heavy for it, Nature was holding on her calm inexorable way, in unmoved and terrible beauty. The stars were rushing in their eternal courses; the tides welled to the level of the last expectant week; the sun was making brilliant day to busy

nations on the other side of the swift earth. The stream of human thought and deed was hurrying and broadening onward. The astronomer was at his telescope; the great ships were laboring over the waves; the toiling eagerness of commerce, the fierce spirit of revolution, were only ebbing in brief rest; and sleepless statesmen were dreading the possible crisis of the morrow. What were our little Tina and her trouble in this mighty torrent, rushing from one awful unknown to another? Lighter than the smallest center of quivering life in the waterdrop, hidden and uncared for as the pulse of anguish in the breast of the tiniest bird that has fluttered down to its nest with the long-sought food, and has found the nest torn and empty.

Here the pathos is not of the sort that Ruskin would term the pathetic fallacy; for this would assume that nature really cared, that storms would sympathize with the heroine's grief and sunbeams smile upon her happiness. Nor is it to be compared with Pascal's shudder over the eternal silences of the infinite spaces, since a bustling world is going about its callous business around her. It does presume the disappearance of God, and consequently the individual feeling of complete psychological isolation. Little Tina seems farther away from the astronomer than from the lost nestlings. Tennyson would wrestle with the problem throughout *"In Memoriam"*: "Are God and Nature then at strife / That Nature lends such evil dreams?" Or are these ostensible cold facts, on the contrary, the material actualities that scientists would confirm? For the romantic poets, licensed dreamers, science had become the encroaching nightmare, the adversary to be warded off by conjuring up the enchantments of storied tradition once more. Blake's couplets had been incantations, if not auguries:

> The atoms of Democritus
> And Newton's particles of light
> Are sands upon the Red Sea shore,
> Where Israel's tents do shine so bright.

Blake was voicing a mystical reaction to Newtonian rationalism; for, as Marjorie Nicolson has demonstrated in her monograph *Newton Demands the Muse* (the title being a quotation from a minor poet, Richard Glover), Newton's *Opticks* had profoundly affected the treatment of light and color in eighteenth-century English poetry.

The painter Benjamin Haydon, notwithstanding, recollects a convivial evening when Lamb and Keats agreed that Newton "had destroyed all the poetry of the rainbow by reducing it to the prismatic colors." Wordsworth, who was present, had played an ambivalent part in the ongoing argument between vitalistic beauty and analytical reason; both sides are forcefully stated in "Expostulation and Reply." He could lament, in the mood of George Eliot over her Tina, a heroine going young to her grave and being "Rolled round in earth's diurnal course, / With rocks, and stones, and trees." (A distinctive feature of Wordsworthian diction is this contrast between the distant and slightly pedantic *diurnal* and the down-to-earth monosyllables: *rocks, stones, trees.*)

Goethe had wrong-headedly devised a color-theory of his own, challenging optical instruments and mathematical physics as well as Newton in person. Yet Wordsworth, recollecting his Cambridge days in *The Prelude,* could pause respectfully before Newton's statue, "The marble index of a mind forever / Voyaging through strange seas of thought alone." And in his preface to *Lyrical Ballads* he pledged that the poet would follow the man of science, whenever the latter's investigations led to a further enlargement of man's consciousness:

> The remotest discoveries of the Chemist, the Botanist, or Mineralogist, will be as proper objects of the Poet's art as any upon which it can be employed, if the time should ever come when these things shall be familiar to us, and the relations under which they are contemplated by the followers of these respective sciences shall be manifestly and palpably material to us as enjoying and respecting beings.

Coleridge, in his retrospective account of the *Lyrical Ballads,* used the term *experiment,* possibly for the first time in literary criticism. He recounted the division of labor between the two poets by attributing to Wordsworth "the power of exciting the sympathy of the reader by a faithful adherence to the truth of nature," while relating his contributions to "the power of giving the interest of novelty by the modifying colors of imagination." At the prosaic extreme was "Goody Blake and Harry Gill," at the exotic "The Rime of the Ancient Mariner." Shakespeare had struck a happy medium, according to Dr. Johnson: "he approximates the remote and familiarizes the wonderful." Storytellers have always acknowledged the double need to contrive a tale that is interesting—which implies being novel, strange, surprising—and to tell it with credibility, so that it sounds like the truth. But the emphasis has tended to oscillate between romantic and realistic poles, between anomaly and familiarity. Aristotle had set the main direction for the West by stressing the importance of representation, the criterion of verisimilitude, the concept of *mimesis*, which Richardson would paraphrase as "copying Nature." The course of the modern European novel, as exemplified by Cervantes, was a repudiation of the medieval romance in the light of an advancing realism. In the longest of the essayistic chapters interspersed through *Tom Jones,* Fielding discusses a topic often considered by his critical predecessors, the Marvellous. "I think," he declares, "that it may very reasonably be required of every writer that he keeps within the bounds of possibility; and still remembers that what is not possible for man to perform, it is scarce possible for man to believe he did perform." Fielding has been credited nonetheless with a work of proto-science-fiction, his facetious *Voyage to the Next World.*

"Nor is possibility alone sufficient to justify us," Fielding continues, "we must keep within the rules of probability." This Aristotelian approach was pressed harder and harder as belief in the supernatural receded or was displaced by an increasingly naturalistic worldview. The Spinozistic indentification of God with nature made it impossible to hold any further faith in miracles—that is, in events that could not be explained by natural causes. "This impulse to believe in the marvellous gradually becomes weaker," wrote the great romancer Scott, significantly while reviewing the tales of the German fantasist, E. T. A. Hoffmann. The Gothic novel had predicated a revival of wonder; and Horace Walpole's *Castle of Otranto* is haunted by spectral marvels which go unexplained with impunity; but Mrs. Radcliffe's *Mysteries of Udolpho* turn out to be all-too-human machinations which can be unmasked by detective-story disclosures. Similarly, the mystery-stories of Charles Brockden Brown beckon us toward pseudo-scientific resolutions; whereas the ironic Hawthorne liked to shade his transcendental enigmas with a penumbra of ambiguity, such as the question of Donatello's ears in *The Marble Faun.* Generally speaking, so long as western culture has been pervaded by the idea of progress, writers have done whatever they could to keep pace with the march of intellect. Professor Nicolson has shown that the animalcules of *Gulliver's Travels* would have been unthinkable without the microscope. When Dryden undertook to dramatize *Paradise Lost,* he began with Adam wakening to consciousness and pronouncing these first words: "Who am I? or from whence? For that I am / *(Rising)* I know because I think." The initial thought of this primordial man—the realization that he must now exist because he has discovered his identity through the process of thinking—marks him as a sophisticated thinker of Dryden's period, a Cartesian rationalist.

In his programmatic book, *L'Avenir de la science,* drafted during the revolutionary ardors of 1848 and published somewhat anticlimactically in 1890, the ex-priest Renan proclaimed that science had become a religion, which would be creating the symbols and solving the problems of the future through its *"sacerdoce rationaliste,"* its community of *savants.* Many influential men of letters proved willing to accept that secular credo. Just as life was being demystified by science, so it would be demythologized by literature. "In my opinion," remarked Flaubert, "the novel should be scientific—that is to say, should be based on probable generalities." Though the qualification may point back toward Aristotle, Flaubert's rigorous professionalism is reflected in his documentary research and stylistic precision. Sainte-Beuve, in his well known review of *Madame Bovary,* suggested that the novelist wielded his pen as his surgical father and brother had been handling their scalpels. But the real exemplar was Balzac, who had presented his *Comédie humaine* as a series of studies in natural history. He had eagerly followed the debate on the interrelationship of animal species between Cuvier and Geoffroy Saint-Hilaire, to whom *Le Père Goriot* is dedicated. In the foreward declaring his intentions for the whole series, Balzac proposed a social taxonomy similar to that of the naturalists. However, in addition to the male and female sexes, he introduced a third category, things. What had been mere background was advanced to the foreground; the function of material objects in men's and women's lives became a major component of Balzac's realism; and, as the nineteenth century developed its metropolitan habitats and technological industries, later novelists would more explicitly register the impact of reification.

Zola, roughly starting out where Balzac left off, and adhering to more radical views of both society and nature, made it his aim to show how men and women were being subordinated to things. A moment ago, when I spoke of *naturalists,* I took the word as an old-fashioned synonym for biological scientists, whether botanists or zoologists. Zola would not have us take it otherwise; *"Le naturalisme,"* he announced, *". . . c'est l'anatomie exacte."* Taking *naturalism* as his novelistic slogan was to intensify the rigor of his philosophical determinism. In the mean time the Darwinian theory had intervened, and its anti-anthropocentric reductionism went even farther to undermine the status of human dignity than the astronomical reductions of the Renaissance. Theodore Dreiser's rising tycoon, Frank Cowperwood, learns the lessons of social Darwinism by watching an aquarium and musing: "Things lived by each other—that was it. Lobsters lived on squid and other things. What lived on lobster? Men, of course! Sure, that was it! And what lived on men?" The answer, of course, is "men." Here in *The Financier* and in its sequel, *The Titan,* there is a struggle for existence at any rate, a Balzacian will to power. The outlook is more Zolaesque, more prone to concentrate upon more passive victims of the environment, in Dreiser's later masterwork, *An American Tragedy.* The downwardly mobile family is there envisaged as "one of the anomalies of psychic and social reflex and motivation such as would tax the skill of not only the psychologist but the chemist and the physicist as well, to unravel." The disaffection of the conditioning milieu serves to reinforce "those rearranging chemisms upon which all the morality and immorality of the world is based." Psychology, as well as ethics, is reduced under such conditions to the irredeemable pessimism of a cosmic shrug.

Zola's mentor had been the eminent physiologist Claude Bernard. "The novelist who studies habits complements the physiologist who studies organs," he commented when Bernard was succeeded by Renan at the Académie Française. Zola looked upon himself as such a novelist, and had found his guide in Bernard's *Introduction à l'étude de la médecine expérimentale.* His manifesto, *Le Roman expérimental,* consists mostly of quotations and paraphrases from that medical treatise, routinely and naïvely making the verbal substitution of *romancier* for *médecin.* Zola believed that he had been employing such exact procedures in his twenty-volume sequence, *Les Rougon-Macquart,* wherein he delineated the patterns of advancement and deterioration through the genealogy of two related families. Now experimentation is controlled observation, as Zola echoed Bernard; yet, in its application to fictional constructs, that notion can be no more than a metaphor. Zola surpassed all previous novelists in his reliance on carefully documented observation; but he had no control over what he observed, whereas his control over what he recorded could be subjective and arbitrary. His presentation of his material, as he elsewhere admitted, was "an aspect of nature viewed through the medium of a temperament." Part of the confusion may derive from the equivocal French noun *expérience,* which signifies both a laboratory test and an acquaintance with life. A novelist tends to be, in T. S. Eliot's phrasing, "expert beyond experience." He can play God with his characters, if he so wishes, determining their hereditary destinies by any set of doctrinaire presuppositions he chooses to espouse. Actually, Zola had no physiological data of any exactitude. He simply made his story-lines conform to certain genetic theories, currently under challenge and subsequently discredited. Hence his method rested not upon induction but on deduction, the very antithesis of scientific empiricism.

In its formal aspect, there is not very much that seems strikingly experimental in Zola's fiction—as contrasted, for instance, with the novelties of technique and style in *Tristram Shandy*. Furthermore, the history of ideas can teach us that Sterne's meandering and fragmented monologue parodied the epistemology of Locke, plus the associations and sensations of eighteenth-century psychology. Given the sensitivity of fiction to its cultural climate, it was bound to reflect the growing assimilation of conceptions shaped by and gathered from science. The reaction could be critical, as in Turgenev's *Fathers and Sons*. There the protagonist Bazarov is a chemist and medical student, a thoroughgoing materialist who despises Pushkin and venerates Bunsen, Liebig, and Büchner, who vivisects frogs and preaches nihilism. Inevitably a conflict between generations provokes a duel in which little is resolved. A parallel dialectic was being argued out across Europe on the educational plane. Matthew Arnold's essay, "Literature and Science," was delivered first as a Rede Lecture, seventy-seven years before C. P. Snow would avail himself of that Cambridge platform to propound his views on the two cultures. Arnold in his turn was replying to T. H. Huxley's "Science and Culture," a plea for introducing more of the sciences into the curriculum. Arnold conceded that educated persons ought to know something about their own bodies and about the corporeal world they inhabited. However, he contended that if they were acquainted with the factual results of scientific investigation, they could leave the experimental methods to specialists. It is evident, in retrospect, that Arnold and Huxley did not totally differ in their basic notions of science. Both of them thought of it as a stable body of solid knowledge, still incomplete and needing to be organized, having been accumulated slowly in the past but lately approaching a fruition of certainty.

"At the end of the nineteenth century," Stanislaw Lem has observed in *The Investigation*, "it was universally believed that we knew almost everything there was to know about the material world, that there was nothing left to do except keep our eyes open and establish priorities.'' No wonder that the simplistic disseminators of such messianic beliefs had expected and even planned a scientific take-over in all fields of human endeavor, as with the positivistic religion of Auguste Comte or the social statics of Herbert Spencer. The exploits of technology, particularly in the United States, urbanized and electrified the ubiquitous landscape. Mark Twain's Sir Boss could stage a confrontation between Yankee know-how and old-world legend; but Huck Finn has been fading into nostalgia, having lighted out from a civilization personified not so much by Aunt Polly as by the teen-age inventor, Tom Swift. The twentieth century seemed to herald a millennium, through its progress-marking expositions and lunar futuramas. It is no accident that the nineteen-twenties, whose lifestyle was shaped by such culture-heroes as Edison, Ford, Burbank, Marconi, and Lindbergh, witnessed the new wave of science-fiction magazines, or that *Amazing Stories* could flaunt the motto: "Extravagant Fiction Today . . . Cold Fact Tomorrow." When Jules Verne criticized H. G. Wells for unduly fantasizing, for not being plausible enough in backing his pseudo-inventions with corroborative detail, Verne was acknowledging the extent to which he and his followers had been working within the realistic conventions. Conrad evoked "the Realities of the Fantastic" in this very connection; Michel Butor would call for their counterpart, *"un fantastique encadré dans un réalisme."* Latterly, with cybernetic systems and nuclear bombs and rockets, reality has been outdoing fantasy and rapidly proceeding from the millennial toward the apocalyptic.

Aldous Huxley, as the literary scion of a scientific dynasty, has commented upon the comparative slowness and uninventiveness of the earlier futurological authors in transcending the undeveloped technologies of their day. To the several examples he has cited, we might add that of Poe in *"Mellonta Tauta,"* where balloons are still the primary means of aerial transportation in the year 2848—a thousand years after the story's date—and the railways have so expanded that they now utilize twelve tracks rather than two. (That, at least, was an optimistic projection.) "Rooted as they are in the facts of contemporary life," Huxley concluded, "the fantasies of even a second-rate writer of modern science-fiction are incomparably richer, bolder, and sharper than the utopias or millennial imaginings of the past." Those developments which we have chiefly been considering were related to an epoch of positivism in science, which bore a special relation to the epoch of realism in literature, as we have seen. This movement has continued, with due allowance for time-lag, well into the present. Yet, away from its near-certitudes, there has been a quantum leap into the more restless epoch of Heisenberg's uncertainty, Gödel's indeterminacy, Einstein's relativity, and the apprehension of bright planets collapsing into black holes. The old and outmoded ideal was one of steady accumulation and continuous progression, filling in the gaps and rounding out the contours of a single, well-defined system, so that Einstein could affirm that nature had been an open book to Newton. But, as Thomas Kuhn has been demonstrating, science moves in intermittent cycles and in uncharted directions. Obviously the positivists of the nineteenth century were basing their presuppositions on paradigms differing from those envisaged by our twentieth-century relativists, and were therefore offering different models to be culturally absorbed or emulated. All that can be confidently predicted, in the face of another scientific revolution, is an utter change in implicit values and sustaining attitudes.

To revert to the novel again is to perceive an analogous shift. Its turning-point has been Joyce's *Ulysses,* which earned immediate notoriety as the *nec plus ultra* of naturalism, but has since been exercising leadership as an introjector of symbolism in fiction. Joyce's youthful surrogate, Stephen Dedalus in *A Portrait of the Artist as a Young Man,* had confessed himself an indifferent member of a college class in physics. Leopold Bloom, the latterday Ulysses, differs from Stephen so diametrically that, when they are finally brought together, they are visualized as respective examples of the artistic and the scientific temperaments. But Bloom, a self-educated common man blandly up-to-date in 1904, can invoke no more than the prevalent commonplaces of popular science. Two physical principles come and go in his mind throughout that crucial day. One is the law of falling bodies ("thirty-two feet per sec"); and the other "parallax," the apparent displacement caused by a change of vantage-point in astronomy. Both have their thematic significances for the symbolic interplay. The chapter that brings the two protagonists *tête-à-tête* over a belated cup of tea, "Ithaca," has been labelled a catechism; but it is much more like an examination paper in its worked-up factuality. Its questions and answers elicit detailed statistics about the flow of water from the reservoir to Bloom's kitchen tap, or the calorific effect of the stove upon the teapot. When the pair exchange their farewells on the doorstep, the starry night is specified in astronomical terminology. Bloom's final—if not uncontested—resting place, his wife's bed, is designated by longitude and latitude. The last line, inadvertently omitted from many editions, is a small black dot suggesting that the earth itself has been whirling off into "the cold of interstellar space."

Here the artistic, not the scientific, temperament, was the demiurge that created a fabulous artifact. If *Ulysses* carried the literal reproduction of daily routine about as far as it could be conveyed in serious prose, it simultaneously opened the way for a renewal of fantasy. Not that the naturalistic movement had ever completely succeeded in grounding the marvellous. Henry James lent his prestigious *cachet* to the composition of ghost stories. The devil makes an appearance in *The Brothers Karamazov,* as does an angel in André Gide's *Faux-monnayeurs,* and God reveals Himself in G. K. Chesterton's detective-story, *The Man Who Was Thursday.* The posthumous emergence of Kafka's fables contributed to the vein of anti-realism. That latitude for the imagination which Hawthorne had requested, and on which he based his distinction between the novel and the romance, is manifest in the writing of such contemporaries as J. L. Borges, Günter Grass, Italo Calvino, and Thomas Pynchon. To collate the three editions of I. A. Richards's *Science and Poetry* (1926, 1935, 1970) is to observe that this sensitive critic, moving from a quasi-positivistic analysis to a neo-romantic defense of poetry, has completely reversed his stand. It may not be impertinent to note that Professor Richards, who had his university training in logic and psychology, has himself become a poet during his elder years. The pace at which the hot facts of our century have outdistanced its anticipatory fictions, has led to suspensions of disbelief far deeper and more widespread than anything Coleridge could have prophesied, in his romantic recoil from the predispositions of eighteenth-century rationalism. A pivotal event was the crisis of 1938, when Orson Welles' broadcast dramatization of an invasion from Mars, as conceived by H. G. Wells, spread panic through whole suburbs of radio listeners.

Another case in the annals of our subject had a genuine cause and an opposite consequence. After the Sputnik entered its first trajectory, as you are doubtless aware, there was a marked—if temporary—decline in the circulation of science-fiction. Reality, on that rare occasion, had come nearer than usual to satisfying man's appetite for amazement. But, although the knowable is necessarily limited, there can be no limits to the unknown; and, for space-opera, the sky itself is not necessarily the limit. The surrounding "mystery of things," to borrow a Shakespearean phrase, is irregularly and sporadically penetrated by reason's lights. This is what makes it so much easier to believe than to doubt, though it is sometimes tempting to speculate or extrapolate; new beliefs are posited upon such speculations and extrapolations, to be either taken on faith or tested by experiment. Whenever institutions or ideologies formed around traditional beliefs are questioned or rejected, then a swarm of esoteric cults seems to creep forth from underground. The Enlightenment, for all its skeptical inclinations, harbored sects of Illuminists, Rosicrucians, and Swedenborgians. During the very years of the French Revolution, a minor playwright and advocate who was participating in it, C. G. T. Garnier, published at Amsterdam a collection of thirty-nine volumes: *Voyages imaginaires, romanesques, merveilleux, allégoriques, amusants, comiques, et critiques: suivis des songes et visions, et des romans cabalistiques.* These included translations of *Robinson Crusoe* first of all, *Gulliver's Travels* (with a French sequel), and *The Life and Adventures of Peter Wilkins* (their once-popular derivate), along with such other pioneering excursions as Voltaire's *Micromégas* and Holberg's *Nils Klim*. It is not without significance that they were intermixed with "visions" and supernatural fantasies, and that Garnier also edited *Le Cabinet des fées*, a forty-one volume collection of fairy tales.

Every work of fiction, in a certain sense, constitutes an extraordinary voyage for its reader. So Tzvetan Todorov maintains in his *Introduction à la littérature fantastique,* and the sweep of the generalization is strengthened if we apply it *a fortiori* to Joyce's *Ulysses*. Travel has furnished a dynamic impetus for civilization itself, and it is their transmigrations which have logged the heterogeneous cultures into an intellectual continuum. It is not surprising when the imaginative curiosity of some self-dispatched voyagers has exceeded any viably geographical itinerary, or when historical explorations—adventurous enough on the surfaces of the earth—have been fancifully extended to subterranean or extraterrestrial regions. Travellers' tales have been proverbially heightened toward comic proportions, what with Lucian, Sir John Mandeville, Cyrano de Bergerac, Baron Münchausen, or Davy Crockett. More humanely, the interest in unexplored territories or in worlds elsewhere has converged with the utopian quest for better worlds. The retrospective outlook was elegiac and pastoral, centering upon a golden age or an earthly paradise. The future prospect, setting its sights from Bacon's *New Atlantis,* is postulated as urban and technocratic. The applications of science were largely seen, through the nineteenth century and somewhat beyond, as a means of ameliorating the quality of life, most optimistically in the utopias of

Bellamy and Wells. But, with the accelerated automation of the twentieth century, utopias have been giving way to dystopias, like the bleak regimes described by Huxley and Orwell—or, more recently and worst of all, the "cacotopia" of Anthony Burgess, *1985*. The idealist, with Plato or More, embodies his ideals in another country, a lost fatherland, a heterocosm. The satirist, disillusioned by his homeland, especially when inhibited by Marxian censorship, can vent his satire on an unmapped domain, as Evgeni Zamyatin did in *We*. The Ukrainian dissenter, Mykola Rudenko, attests: "It was science-fiction that turned me into a 'renegade'."

Such Victorian prophets as Morris and Butler had sought guidelines for the future by turning back to the past. *News from Nowhere* supplanted factories with crafts and relocated townspeople in the countryside. *Erewhon* reverted to its antipodean pastoralism by staging a neo-Luddite revolt and sabotaging the oppressive machines. More currently *A Clockwork Orange,* if I read its Russo-English dialect correctly, has been protesting against the behavioral engineering of such a utopia as B. F. Skinner's *Walden Two*. Since the most violent delinquency may be regarded as an assertion of free will, Mr. Burgess seems to believe, it is morally preferable to a social rehabilitation programmed through conditioned reflexes. A comparable dialectic was provoking its counterstatements more than a hundred years before, when the Goncourt brothers jotted down their reactions to an American writer just translated:

> After having read Poe. Something heretofore unnoted in criticism, a new literary world, portents of twentieth-century literature. Science as miracle, algebraic fiction, a lucid and morbid literature. More poetry, imagination with thrusts of analysis. Zadig as police investigator, Cyrano de Bergerac studying astronomy with Arago. Somewhat monomaniacal.—Things playing more roles than people; love yielding to deductions and to other sources of ideas, phrases, stories, and general interest; the basis of the novel displaced and transposed from the heart to the head and from passion to intellect; drama in liquefaction.

The fraternal diarists did not go so far as to prophesy the invention of the hydrogen bomb, but the faceless landscape they foresaw looks very much as if it had been dehumanized by one. Nor can we deny that their preview has, to some extent, come to pass. "Men and landscape interfuse," as Mr. Aldiss perceives so clairvoyantly:

"Machines predominate." The Philosophes, though they did not dream of bionic androids, could conceive the human body as a mechanism: La Mettrie's *"L'homme machine."* The concentration on things, evinced by Balzac and intensified by Zola, has culminated among the authors of the *nouveau roman:* for example, in the *chosisme* of *La Jalousie,* where Robbe-Grillet's cinematic focus is less upon the men and women within a given room than on the spot left by a crushed centipede on the wall. Comparable to the impressions of the Goncourts were those of the French novelist who became the most successful of Poe's emulators. Jules Verne also sensed a certain coldness in "this positivist of a man," which he blamed on the regimented materialism of Poe's native American surroundings. Yet the latter characteristic, too, was a source of strength and originality, for it had enabled him to confront and dispel all vestiges of the supernatural: "He claims to explain everything by physical law, which he is even ready to invent, if need be."

When Verne went on to deplore Poe's alcoholic tendencies, he failed to recognize that Poe's overemphasis on "ratiocination" was like the heavy drinker's effort to convince his sober interlocutors that he is in a rational frame of mind. It is ironic—in view of such emotional Gallic responses—that, when Poe came to portray his past master of deduction and cerebration, he could not make him other than a Frenchman: M. Auguste Dupin. For the mysteries Poe conjured up there would invariably be *éclaircissements,* practical solutions to his riddles, enigmas, and parlor tricks. He enjoyed playing the self-appointed debunker of other people's hoaxes, as with "Maelzel's Chess-Player," where his exposure of an actual person concealed within the machinery of the spurious automaton constituted a Bergsonian victory of the living over the mechanical. (It is still not possible to program a computer for meeting the virtual infinitude of contingencies that could theoretically arise in a game of chess.) Poe's most ambitious undertaking, "Eureka," originally presented as a two-hour lecture on cosmogony, is nothing less than an attempt to solve the riddle of the universe. Prefacing the printed version, Poe offered it to the reader as a prose poem rather than a scientific treatise, for its beauty rather than its truth. There was not much Keatsian equivalence. On the one hand, the pseudo-professional patter borrowed from Alexander von Humboldt and the cosmographers was hardly the stuff of poetry. On the other, Poe was well advised in not pretending to be a scientist. A. H. Quinn, his loyal if pedestrian biographer, managed to extract a letter from Sir Arthur Eddington, making polite allowances for cranky amateurism and for contemporaneous misconception, while conceding some amount of credit to a romantic poet who was sufficiently interested to dabble in questions now under scrutiny by the astrophysicists.

The predominant intention of "Eureka," which could not be adjudged as either true or false, was to unify the concepts of spirit and matter, of time and space, through a single-minded commitment to the integrity of the imagination. Paul Valéry's oracular essay about it may tell us more about himself than Poe: how, on discovering it at the age of twenty, while vacillating between a career in letters and one in mathematics, it struck him with all the force of a cosmic vocation (*"voilà mon premier univers"*). And the testimonial concludes by rounding an interdisciplinary circle: "IN THE BEGINNING WAS THE FABLE!" It will always be there." The more we learn about intelligence, the more we respect its permutations and varieties, and the less we feel inclined to subdivide it crudely into two categorical opposites. "There is no science without fancy and no art without facts," as Vladimir Nabokov has written in *Ada,* that amorphous novel which includes—among so many other outlandish things—a burlesque of what the author (himself a part-time entomologist) preferred to label "physics-fiction." What we consider occult is by definition what we do not understand, and this may well expose our own ignorance in contradistinction to the expertise of the genuine professionals. But science, unsupported by direct conversance with the experimental evidence, has no more positive standing in our minds than magic; hobbits have much the same espistemological status as robots; and there is a philosophical inference to be drawn from the intermingling of science-fiction with fantasy, not excluding religious allegory and medievalized folklore, on our bookshelves and in our conference. Carlyle's formula, "natural supernaturalism," has been fruitfully revived by M. H. Abrams, and it might well be transferred from romanticism to a newer blend of pantheism, not so much a *mystique* as a resurrection of miracles without the intervention of an established God.

"Not everyone can be Lord God *tout court,* a creator of autonomous worlds, and a writer most certainly cannot," Stanislaw Lem has warned us, in a recent review of a nonexistent book. The more improbable the writer's world, the less explainable is its relation to ours—or rather, the Lord's. Science abhors transcendence, naturally enough, and transposes the supernatural to the paranormal. When the Brobdingnagian professors who examined Gulliver ended by classifying him as a freak of nature, *lusus naturae,* Swift's ironic conclusion was that they were "disdaining the old evasion of occult causes" and finding "a wonderful solution of all difficulties, to the unspeakable advancement of human knowledge." In other words, they were getting rid of the problem by sweeping it under the rug. The rigorous empiricist would take the stance of Newton: "*Hypotheses non fingo.* All that is not deduced from phenomena is hypothesis, and hypotheses—be they metaphysical, physical, mechanical, or occult—have no place in experimental philosophy." I cite the famous dictum in Newton's original Latin because the verb is suggestively linked to my subject-matter. *Fingo* here is best translated "fabricate." Thus it has the same ambiguous connotations as the Greek *poíesis,* which can mean either making something or making something up. Even more to the point, its participial substantive is the etymological precedent for our word *fiction.* Newton equated hypothesizing with fabrication or fiction: "I do not fabricate hypotheses." The Newtonian scholar, Alexandre Koyré, has pointed out that on inconsistent occasions Newton himself made use of hypothetical propositions, but that he consistently reserved the specific expression for pejorative comment on the researches of rival scientists. Modern scientific procedure, as formulated by Henri Poincaré in *La Science et l'hypothèse,* while concurring with Newton on the necessity for experimental verification, would concede that hypotheses could perform heuristic functions.

In that respect, the ultimate cosmos of science is not so far removed from the artificial microcosms of literature. "A fictive covering," Wallace Stevens has written, "Weaves always glistening from the heart and mind." And within the domain of fiction, as we have been taking notice, the fabrications of science are not so far removed from the fantasies of the literary—or, beyond the self-consciously literary, the traditional and popular—imagination. The Russian folklorist, Vladimir Propp, has worked out a *Morphology of the Folktale* which, since it breaks down narrative into its most elemental components and schematized relationships, need not vary much from one genre to another. It could be applied almost as readily to the sophistications of Proust as to the simplicities of the brothers Grimm. The dean of American folklorists, Stith Thompson, from a very different angle of observation, has compiled his *Motif-Index of Folk-Literature.* Since he has ordered his vast range of materials by a thematic scheme of classification, it is revealing to observe the principal themes: cosmogony, the creation of life, arcane knowledge, magical transactions, otherworldly journeys, ogres and ordeals, raising the dead, foreseeing and controlling the future. What are these folkloristic categories but the standard situations of science-fiction? Of course, we must allow for a certain amount of temporal adaptation. Pseudo-science may be counted upon to have modernized the technique of necromancy; but thaumaturgy continues to work its recurrent wonders, no more wonderful when manifested in witches' cauldrons than in physicists' cyclotrons. Personally, I remain enough of a skeptical rationalist to feel somewhat uneasy over the cultural currents that have been remystifying and remythologizing our precarious century. Our technorevolutions seem to foster, not so much a rule of reason, as an efflorescence of credulity. Perhaps the last word should be left to P. T. Barnum.

Incorporating Divinity: Platonic Science Fiction in the Middle Ages

Kent T. Kraft

One of the cruxes of science fiction criticism is the problem of delimiting the genre. At what point in literary history can science fiction be said to begin? Is it a literary mode that can arise in any age, impelled by man's eternal need to speculate on what lies beyond currently accepted limits of perception? Or is it the specific product of certain unique historical conditions—of a scientific age perhaps where science is not simply "love of knowledge" but rather a search to know? Brian Aldiss, for example, considers the rise of science fiction as an essentially Romantic phenomenon: "Science fiction is the search for a definition of man and his status in the universe which will stand in our advanced but confused state of knowledge (science) and is characteristically cast in the Gothic or post-Gothic mould."[1] The Middle Ages, then, where both man's being and his place in the universe were primarily fixed entities, and where science was less "confused" speculation than knowable truth, would seem (if we accept Aldiss' definition) completely refractory to the development of such a form. Darko Suvin, however, presents a view of the genre that allows for much broader origins: "[science fiction] should be defined as a fictional tale determined by the hegemonic literary device of a *locus* and/or *dramatis personae* that (1) are *radically or at least significantly different from the empirical times, places, and characters of* 'mimetic' or 'naturalist' fiction but (2) are nonetheless—to the extent that SF differs from other 'fantastic' genres . . . simultaneously perceived as *not impossible* within the cognitive (cosmological and anthropological) norms of the author's epoch."[2] What I shall describe as "Platonic science fiction" fits this interpretive framework. Considered his-

torically what position does such a form occupy? In its double static nature—governed by norms that are not only "cognitive" but rhetorical as well—how can this form be more than a starting point, a point in reaction to which science fiction as we know it begins? Suvin's theoretical relativism is itself perhaps only a screen. For, when he begins his historical survey of forms, what he describes (in terms of his central relationship between empirical and "alternative" space) is a foreshortening process that accelerates in the eighteenth century ("SF begins turning to a *time* into which the author's age might evolve") and seems to peak in Aldiss' nineteenth century. As we shall see, however, these medieval narrative structures, though conceived within a pre-Copernican frame, do develop historically. What is more, they seem to evolve in the manner Suvin describes—as speculative worlds they appear to tend toward, if not identity with empirical place and character, at least a greater degree of contiguity with them. But the matter is more subtle yet. The type of "fabulous narrative" that arises in this particular matrix, because of its built-in resistance to dynamic change, may form a mode of speculative fiction that is both alternate and parallel to the one both Suvin and Aldiss seek to isolate.

Much of the literature of a speculative nature in the Middle Ages is influenced by a curious thematic proscription. This latter appears in a source that may at first sight seem strange to us moderns. Macrobius, the fourth-century Neoplatonist who wrote an encyclopedic commentary on Cicero's *Dream of Scipio,* introduces his work by establishing a series of distinctions between various sorts of narratives. There are *fabulae,* or "fables," he tells us, that are purely entertaining, and there are others that serve a moral or didactic purpose. Of this second group, some, like Aesop's fables, deal with fictitious material. Others use the techniques of fictional narrative to speak about true things, including the truths of natural philosophy or what in today's terms would be the domain of natural science.[3]

Having established a category for philosophical speculation (he calls it *narratio fabulosa,* or "fabulous narrative"), Macrobius is now very careful about delineating precisely what sort of phenomena may appropriately be dealt with in such a narrative. "Philosophers," he says, "do not admit fabulous matter . . . into every disputation; but they tend to use it when speaking of the soul, of the aerial or ethereal powers, or of the other gods."[4] Thus Macrobius permits fictive discussion of such significant features of the late antique cosmos as the spirits or *daemones* that inhabit the air below the moon and, more importantly, the planets and the elements (like Cicero before him, Macrobius regards these as divine entities).

There is, however, a limit to what may be discussed in a fictional philosophical narrative, for "when a treatise dares to aspire to the highest, the chiefest God of all [who is called by the Greeks the Good (ταγαθον) and the First Cause (πρῶτον αἴτιον)], or to that Mind, which the Greeks call *Nous*, containing the original concepts of things, the *ideai* [that is, the Platonic Forms or Ideas], that Mind born of and proceeding from the supreme God—when, I repeat, the authors speak of the supreme God and Mind, they do not touch upon anything fabulous."[5] A certain tactfulness, in other words, inhibits us from treating supreme religious truths (or, at least, those of Neoplatonism) in a fictional or allegorical narrative. Discourse at this level demands a shift to the mode of analogy, for here we are dealing with things that surpass human comprehension and that elude our customary faculties of expression. Similes and metaphors, such as Plato's comparison of the Good to the sun of the physical world, must serve where fabulous narrative cannot. Indeed, "it is wholly unlawful for fables to enter here."[6]

The two examples of proper philosophical fables upon which Macrobius bases his argument—the Myth of Er at the end of Plato's *Republic* and the *Dream of Scipio*—naturally satisfy his criteria. Although the human soul and the constitution of the universe are of major importance in the narratives, the *Nous* and the supreme deity do not appear at all in Plato's fable and are touched on only incidentally by Cicero. In both tales the chief focus is rather the condition of the human soul in the afterlife and the nature of the cosmos in which it dwells, and both include an elaborate description of the arrangement of the planets and the spheres that bear them. But between the Myth of Er and the *Dream of Scipio*, an important shift of perspective occurs. The universe that in Plato's *Republic* serves as a model to be contemplated abstractly changes to a field for movement and action. Cicero's work thereby sets the stage for a curious array of later "fabulous narratives" in which various allegorical personages make their way up through the heavens to the limits of the universe. Eventually, compelled by theological necessity, their authors will violate Macrobius' injunctions and populate these outer realms not only with the Neoplatonic pantheon that Macrobius prohibits but with a galaxy of Christian "divinities" as well.

It would be difficult to call the Myth of Er a piece of science fiction, even if we were to limit our definition of the genre to something like "a fictitious narrative whose theme is derived in large part from speculation on established or hypothetical scientific principles." The story reports a vision of the afterlife by the Pamphylian soldier, Er, who has been killed in battle but who is mysteriously restored to life again twelve days later. Most of it comprises an allegorical account of the judgment of the just and the unjust souls, their rewards and punishments, and the lottery that determines their human reincarnations every thousand years. Its setting is the realm of the dead, a vague land containing the meadow where souls are judged, the plain of Lethe with its river of forgetfulness, and a strange place where the souls are granted what J. A. Stewart has called "a vision within the larger vision of the whole Myth of Er."[7]

Here Er and his companions see a vast shaft of light that reaches from one pole of the universe to the other and that bears what Plato calls the "Spindle of Necessity." This instrument, though resting upon the knees of Necessity and turned by her and her daughters, the Fates, is itself not nearly so fantastic a construction as is the rest of the tale. It is, in effect, a miniature version of the universe or, as F. M. Cornford put it, "a primitive orrery in a form roughly resembling a spindle."[8] The shaft corresponds to the polar axis of the cosmos; at its base is a whorl made up of eight hemispheres "fitting into one another like a nest of bowls."[9] This represents, in cross section, the spherical configuration of the universe devised by Plato's disciple Eudoxus.[10] The eight nested whorls, which move with varying speeds, model the spheres of the stars and planets that revolve about the earth. A Siren stands upon the rim of each whorl, singing a single note, and the eight notes of the eight Sirens produce Plato's version of the music of the spheres.

The overall impression one gets from Er's account and from the cosmological "vision within the vision" is that of passive, theoretical contemplation. Er himself serves merely as an observer. He is not really dead, not caught up in fears of punishment and hopes of reward. Even those dwelling in the afterworld are aware of this; he is told to remember what he sees and hears, since he is to report on this other world when he returns to the living, and he is not permitted to drink of the waters of Lethe and gain a new birth as are the other souls. The dispassion of Er's narration, already distanced and removed from the realm of action, is enhanced by the introduction of the spindle, itself a *theorema*, an object for contemplation like the initiatory spectacles in the mystery cults. As Er gazes upon the souls gazing upon this model of the world, we, as readers, are presented less with a speculation on the possibilities of the universe than with a projected image or symbol of its operations. We see the universe at a remove, neatly opened for inspection, but are not immediately subject to the consequences of its laws.

Where Plato shapes a mythical image of the universe, Cicero, in the *Dream of Scipio,* creates a myth whose meaning is derived largely from the spatial framework of the cosmos itself, where the position of the observer within the cosmos determines the true significance of such conventionally important items as planets, empires, and the works of man. Scipio, we recall, has spent the evening talking about his grandfather with Masinissa, king of Numidia. Later, after "a sleep much deeper than was usual"[11] comes upon him, he is visited in a dream by his grandfather, Africanus the Elder. Rapt to a point somewhere high above the earth, he sees first Carthage and then the earth itself as small and insignificant, while the spheres of the planets and the fixed stars loom large before him. Africanus uses this physically elevated standpoint to describe the geographic disposition of the earth and to discourse upon the vanity of earthly fame and glory. The sphere of human action is pitifully small when contrasted with the immensity of the cosmos, and our lives upon the earth ephemeral when compared with the measure of celestial time.[12]

Although Cicero uses virtually the same physical organization for his universe as Plato does, there are some important differences in his treatment of it that bring the *Dream of Scipio* a bit closer than the Myth of Er to what Suvin calls science fiction—a world still radically different from empirical reality, yet losing its fantastic existence, gradually being accommodated within the cosmological and anthropological norms of the author's epoch. Most obvious, of course, is the shift in perspective that follows the narrator from the surface of the earth to an elevated position in the cosmos. This shift occasions not only a change in physical standpoint, which we as readers follow in our imaginations, but a change in moral standpoint as well. Africanus underlines the necessity for this change when he reprimands Scipio for turning his eyes back on earth: "Keep rather your eyes upon these things of the heavens, scorning those of mankind."[13] Scipio, then, unlike Er, is a participant, an actor on the stage of the universe. He does not regard the cosmos with mathematical abstraction; his viewpoint changes as he moves within it, and his moral commitments alter, not merely as a result of observing the fate of the souls of those who have died, but more directly as a consequence of his new physical perspective on things.

Cicero almost seems to pose a fundamental question of science fiction: If I assume that such and such is so, what circumstances will necessarily ensue? If I assume that the universe is spherical and of such and such a size and that I have moved to the level of, let us say, Jupiter, then will the earth and the moon seem correspondingly smaller and the other planets and stars correspondingly larger? It is the same question that Kepler, in a different cognitive framework, will ask himself in 1593 while a student at Tübingen: "How would the phenomena occurring in the heavens appear to an observer stationed on the moon?"[14] Kepler's answer, while considerably more sophisticated in its astronomy and mathematics than Cicero's, is cast in a very similar mold and eventually makes its way into print as his *Dream, or Posthumous Work on Lunar Astronomy*.[15] It is perhaps more "accurate" speculation than the *Dream of Scipio* is, since some of its predictions—for example, of what will happen to a human body leaving the influence of the earth's gravity—were later to be corroborated, but its principle is the same.

Interestingly, in this new context of moral and physical involvement by the narrator in another, speculative space, the *Dream of Scipio*, despite its obvious commitment to a fixed world view, seems less a product of fancy (as Lucian's later heavenly voyage in *A True History*, for instance, most certainly is) than of the speculative scientific imagination. Cicero does not create a fabulous Spindle of Necessity; his spheres produce music mechanically, by their relative size and motion, not by the melodious chants of appended Sirens. Where Plato offers us a complex metaphor, a mythic image of the human soul's relation to the universe's workings, Cicero presents us with a clear proposition. Given the cosmos as it is, multisphered, immense, yet ultimately rational and logically ordered, and given the proper point from which to view it, certain obvious spiritual and ethical considerations must emerge. The *Dream of Scipio* is a clean working-out of a given understanding of the world—not extrapolation from hypothesis, but a making evident of how things are.

Associated with Cicero's unadorned account of the universe as a framework for traveling are the natural limitations he sets upon philosophical topics, the limitations Macrobius will later take as proscriptive. Since he is not concerned with creating a fabulous image or a symbolic representation of a truth too complex to be expressed in a composite metaphor, Cicero consigns not only his discussion of God but also that of the soul and the soul's motion to a straightforward philosophical exposition. Indeed, even the discourse on the soul that he puts in the mouth of Africanus at the end of the *Dream of Scipio* is, as Macrobius himself points out, a literal translation of a logical argument from Plato's *Phaedrus*. But where Macrobius later sees the restrictions that Cicero imposes on his theme as a sign of pious reserve, in the context of the *Dream of Scipio* itself, his decisions are motivated less by religious considerations than by practical aesthetics. There is simply no place in the basically physical account that Cicero gives for allegorical personifications of Platonic divinities. Cicero is creating an allegory only in the vaguest sense; his chief concern is with the moral and didactic consequences of a clear understanding of a well-defined cosmos.

One of the most influential and complex versions of the celestial voyage in the early Middle Ages was Martianus Capella's *Marriage of Philology and Mercury*. Written in the first half of the fifth century, this encyclopedic account of the seven liberal arts is framed in a fanciful allegorical narrative. Here the learned and attractive Philology, chosen by Mercury to be his bride, makes her way to the upper reaches of the heavens for the marriage festival. After first vomiting forth countless tomes on geometry, music, and the other arts that have been weighing her down, she becomes immaterial enough for her celestial ascent. Borne aloft in a palanquin by Attention, Wakefulness, and various other personages, Philology passes sphere after planetary sphere until she reaches the abode of Jupiter in the Milky Way, near the outer limit of the universe. There a throng of gods, spirits, and the apotheosized souls of poets and philosophers have gathered for the ceremony, itself a mere preface to Martianus' long disquisition on the liberal arts.

Like Cicero, Martianus makes the universe a scaffold upon which to suspend his arguments. His aim, however, is not to convey those philosophical truths that follow naturally from the shift from an earthly to a cosmic perspective. What he requires is a vast yet ordered structure full of niches, lodging places that will accommodate his enormous store of learning. Juno, for example, upon welcoming Philology in the upper air, explains to her the nature of the inhabitants of the universe. These range from the pure fiery spirits that dwell in the ether in the region of the stars to the earthbound members of our own species. The intermediary zones, however, are fully populated by such beings as the several degrees of semidivine demons (*daemones*) who live between the sun and the moon; the lesser, more material entities that dwell in the air and vapors below the moon; and the fauns, nymphs, satyrs, and *silvani* that inhabit those places on the earth that are inaccessible to man.

Where Cicero achieves a vision of immediate moral force from the spacious vistas that he places before Scipio's eyes, Martianus evokes the happy *plenum* of the learned pedant. His universe is full and populous; space and being correspond, so that everything has its place, form, and a suitable commentary on it. The effect is analogous to that produced by the mnemonic systems of the ancient art of memory, where an imaginary house or palace becomes the storehouse for mental objects that the mnemonist has associated with various items he wishes to remember in sequence. In order to recover the items at the appropriate moment—when the time comes, for instance, to give a speech or lecture—he simply takes a mental stroll through the imagined edifice. Room after room then discloses its contents, as the spatial pattern of the house orders and arranges the images that unfold to the memory in the linear sequence of time. So Quintilian, in the *Institutio oratoria,* advises us to memorize the pattern of a (Roman) house and to associate the things we want to remember with such objects as an anchor or a weapon or a similar device:

> These signs are then arranged as follows. The first notion is placed, as it were, in the forecourt; the second, let us say, in the atrium; the remainder are placed in order all around the impluvium, and committed not only to bedrooms and parlours, but even to statues and the like. This done, when it is required to revive the memory, one begins from the first place to run through all, demanding what has been entrusted to them, of which one will be reminded by the image. Thus, however numerous the particulars which it is required to remember, all are linked to one another as in a chorus nor can what follows wander from what has gone before to which it is joined, only the preliminary labour of learning being required.[16]

Similarly, Martianus' universe offers the mental security of known spaces, where each idea has a "local habitation and a name." Admittedly, Martianus has garnered his concepts far afield, and the *Marriage of Philology and Mercury* occasionally suffers from a rampant eclecticism. But the entire structure of the work is nonetheless a natural consequence of Martianus' encyclopedic intentions. Where Macrobius creates an elaborate cosmographic commentary on Cicero, transforming what is basically a didactic myth into a Neoplatonic treatise on pneumatology, astronomy, and geography, Martianus fashions the universe anew to make room for a larger exposition. His ornate (one is tempted to say "baroque") cosmos with its eclectic constituency, where Roman deities, Presocratic philosophers, and epic poets hobnob together in the heavens, is nonetheless highly ordered and structured, like the compendious accounts of the liberal arts that complete the work. Indeed, one of the best summaries of Martianus' own practices as poetic demiurge or cosmic fabricator might be his own comments on the "precepts of memorization," which he treats briefly in his discussion of rhetoric:

> . . . it is order which sustains the precepts of memory. These (precepts) are to be pondered upon in well-lighted places in which the images of things [and the representations of ideas] are to be placed. For example (to remember) a wedding you may hold in mind a girl veiled with a wedding-veil; or a sword, or some other weapon, for a murderer; which images as it were deposited (in a place) the place will give back to memory. . . . if the material is lengthy, being divided into parts it may more easily stick (in the memory). It is useful to place *notae* [symbols or marks, perhaps symbolic images] against single points which we wish to retain.[17]

This predilection for the image as an organizing principle underlies Martianus' peculiar creativity. It is reflected, not only in his elaborate allegorical depictions of the Seven Liberal Arts and in his graphic portrayals of the gods, the Graces, the Muses, and such personages as Philosophy, Wisdom, and Philology herself, but in the stations of the cosmos as well. The planet Saturn, which Philology reaches after basking in the "jovial" light of Jupiter, *is* the ancient god: "He wore now the face of a dragon, now the gaping jaws of a lion, now a crest made of the teeth of a boar. In his raging fury he caused horror and destruction, and his power was reckoned to exceed all others according as the size of his circle exceeded theirs."[18] More than any other element of Martianus' artistry, this love of the image is what ultimately makes his universe irreal and fantastic. As the "iconographic frame of mind" (to borrow a phrase from Angus Fletcher),[19] the reductive consciousness of allegory, imposes itself upon the accepted structure of the world, it turns the world itself into an artifact of the imagination. In more modern allegorical science fiction, such as that of David Lindsay or of C. S. Lewis, the universe as we know it is similarly subjected to the claims of the idea or the image, and worlds are created, not to conform to a consistent internal order but to express symbolically the demands of a philosophical stance. Here, in the *Marriage*, the clear, spheric simplicity of Scipio's cosmos, with its enormous spaces and vast harmonies, has been transformed by a visual fascination with the principle of plenitude. What might exist in the heavens, for Martianus, *does* exist, wrapped in symbolic garb.

In some ways Martianus' concern with the image or symbol brings him closer to Plato than to Cicero. Although he does use the cosmos as a backdrop for Philology's allegorical ascent, he, like Plato (and like many modern science fiction writers) is also captivated by the idea of simulacra or models of the universe. And, as in Plato's depiction of the Spindle of Necessity, the passages in which Martianus describes these miniature models of the world are separated from the rest of the text by a form of rhetorical ecphrasis (the technique whereby a work of art, a building, or even a city is elaborately delineated and described).[20] We find, for example, that Astronomy appears before the heavenly assembly in a magical manner, rather like the Good Witch of the North in *The Wizard of Oz:*

> Before their eyes a vision appeared, a hollow ball of heavenly light, filled with transparent fire, gently rotating, and enclosing a maiden within. Several planetary deities, especially those which determine men's destinies, were bathed in its glare, the mystery of their behavior and orbits revealed. Even the fabric of the celestial sphere shone forth in the same flashing light.[21]

More mysterious still is a carved globe that rests before the throne of Juno. It is used by Jupiter in determining the affairs of men and bears a striking resemblance to Jorge Luis Borges' "Aleph":

> It had been so made out of a compound of all the elements that nothing that is believed to be in nature was missing from it. On it were all the sky, air, the seas, all the different things on earth and the barriers of Tartarus: cities, crossroads, every kind of living thing, in species and in genus, could be counted there. This sphere seemed to be an image and model of the world. The daily actions of each and all the people of all nations appeared in this as in a mirror.[22]

Both of these representations of the cosmos reflect a state of mind in which vision is a predominant cognitive faculty and the universe is both made accessible and, as it were, held at bay. Lest we make too much of this visual distancing, however, it would be good to mention a third passage, in which Martianus depicts a miniature world. It is presented to Philology by Immortality, and resembles an egg. Its outside "shone, being anointed with saffron; within that, it seemed transparent with void and a white humor, and then something more solid at the center."[23] Peter Dronke takes this to be an instance of the representation of the universe as "world-egg" and finds numerous later writers who use a similar image.[24] What is remarkable here is that Philology treats this gift like a real egg and gobbles it down. She then finds herself both refreshed and released from worldly concerns, ready for the heavenly journey. By consuming the universe, then, she becomes mistress of its ways. Martianus, I would suggest, is here making a subtle criticism of his own methods: incorporating the universe may be a better way of having it than knowing it or seeing it.

It should be clear from the discussion thus far that Martianus has succeeded in treating, in a very fabulous narrative indeed, the philosophical topics permitted by Macrobius. But what of those that were prohibited, God and the Mind or *Nous?* Here Macrobius' eclecticism raises a problem. Although Richard Johnson writes that "The Marriage admirably exemplifies the confluence of religious traditions in the late Roman Empire and the role of decayed Neoplatonism in blending the streams,"[25] it is this very syncretism that makes it difficult to determine exactly what religious views Martianus held and what theological elements he is vesting in allegorical guise. In general, Jupiter has the role of highest deity. At one point he calls Mercury "the loyal messenger and spokesman of my mind, the sacred *Nous.*"[26] The obvious conclusion should be that Jove is an allegorical representation of God or the One and Mercury similarly represents the *Nous,* or at least a direct emanation from it. Philology, however, addresses Apollo in the following words: "Hail, true face of the gods, countenance of the Father; your number is 608, and your three letters form the holy name and sign of Mind."[27] Leaving aside the numerology and alphabetic mystification, there still seems to be a definite equivalence being made now between Apollo and the divine *Nous.* Later, at the beginning of the discourse on geometry (Book VI), Martianus himself addresses Minerva as "the pinnacle of reason, the holy Mind of gods and men,"[28] so that *three* deities share this one attribute.

As if this were not enough confusion, Philology also calls Apollo "the exalted power of the Father Unknown, . . . source of Mind."[29] We *know* Jupiter; who, then, is the "Father Unknown"? A slight clue comes soon after when we discover that Philology, scanning the universe from its star-laden periphery, "was aware that the god who was the father of such a work and so great a system had withdrawn even from the very acquaintance of the gods, for she knew that he had passed beyond the felicity that is itself beyond this world, and he rejoiced in an empyrean realm of pure understanding."[30] One way of reconciling these apparent discrepancies might be to follow Johnson's suggestion that "this blend of Neoplatonism and Olympian religion does not necessarily involve a contradiction; it simply pushes the hierarchy of being one stage higher, postulates one or more deities of more exalted status, and fits the irrational Olympian figures into an intellectually defensible philosophic system."[31] From this viewpoint, the "Father Unknown" would serve as the transcendent source of Jupiter and the other Olympians, as well as the creator of the world. And, since he is totally extramundane, there is no danger that Martianus is violating Macrobius' injunctions by personifying the One.

Yet there remains the fact that Jupiter governs all creation, and that Mercury, Apollo, and Minerva are identified with the *Nous*. I believe there is an alternate hypothesis to account for these apparent anomalies, one that derives from Martianus' own attitude toward the cosmos and toward his work. We have seen that for him the universe is a great hall of memory, full of symbolic figures and personages. Now, there is always the possibility of walking through that hall more than once, or stepping back and taking another look at what we have just been gazing at. What we see the second time around may not be exactly the same as the first time, because the symbols in the hall can have more than just one meaning. That is their value and their limitation.

Jove and the other Olympians attract ideas because of their symbolic status. Mercury is at once eloquence, which longs to be joined to learning (Philology); the ardent anthropomorphic suitor who wanders in search of a bride; the messenger of Jove; a planet having certain determined characteristics; and the Neoplatonic Mind. Apollo, likewise, is a long-haired prophet who sits on a cliff and disposes good and ill winds for men; the sun that shines in the heavens; a composite figure for Serapis, Horus, Osiris, Attis, and Adonis; and, again, the Neoplatonic Mind.[32] Minerva, besides being an armored goddess, Wisdom, Reason, and Mind, can also be hailed as "loftier than Jove" because she represents the furthest reaches of the ether.[33] It would be valid to assign any one of their attributes to

Mercury, Apollo, or Minerva. That Martianus applies all of them is simply an indication of the wealth of ideational content that these symbolic figures can contain. They are, to use the words of Martianus in his passage on memorizing, *imagines sententiarum,* or "representations of ideas." Once a concept is embodied, once Mercury and Apollo and Minerva are available as "symbolic images," they remain available to attract further concepts.[34] God and the *Nous* are part of Martianus' mental furnishings; it is only natural that they attach themselves to a suitable preexistent form.

What appears to be Martianus' fabulous depiction of the One and the *Nous*—that is, their rather confused identification with Jove, Minerva, Mercury, and Apollo—may after all have a simple explanation, one that exonerates him from any offense against Macrobius. Martianus is well aware of the supreme status of the One itself. He consigns it (in the form of the "Father Unknown") to the realm of the empyrean, an apparently impenetrable region beyond the outermost bound of the physical universe. He is thus, in intention at least, putting the One "off limits" for a fabulous treatment. Yet to the mind of Martianus the encyclopedist, this extramundane assignment cannot suffice. While there are images available to express the One and its relation to the *Nous,* he will use them. The *Nous* is the sun of the intelligible world to the Neoplatonist; why not then link it with Phoebus Apollo? And what better figure for the emanation of the One through the *Nous* than the winged messenger Mercury? It is not that Martianus is consciously striving to create allegorical embodiments for these spiritual entities; rather, he has suitable figures at hand and cannot resist uniting them with ideas in search of a form.

The last work that we shall consider stems from the period when the philosophical tenets and literary theories of Neoplatonism underwent their first great revival. It was written in France in the mid-twelfth century by one of C. S. Lewis' favorite authors, Bernardus Silvestris, and incorporates a world view so apparently heterodox that modern critics have often labeled it pagan, pantheistic, or, at best, dualist.[35] Entitled *De mundi universitate* or, more often, *Cosmographia,* the work is divided into two sections, *Megacosmus* and *Microcosmus.* Its theme is the creation of the world and of that "little world" that mirrors it, man.

Bernardus has as model and guide the outline of the universe presented by Plato in his own cosmogonic myth, the *Timaeus.* One of the few Platonic dialogues known in the Middle Ages, the *Timaeus* had been transmitted, like the *Dream of Scipio,* through a Neoplatonic commentator—in this case, Chalcidius. Like Macrobius, Chalcidius is a dissector of myth. As Brian Stock writes:

> His commentary is a comprehensive exposition of the *Timaeus*, taking each separate theme in the myth as a topic for synthesizing the thought of a number of ancient schools. The reader is thus presented with an entirely different literary form from the original. While based upon the idea of myth, the commentary turns the notion around and presents instead a demythologization.[36]

In other words, Chalcidius "deconstructs" the universe Plato has constructed in his fabulous narrative. Bernardus in turn constructs from this exegetical material a new myth, similar to Plato's in some ways but incorporating as well the thought of various Neoplatonic philosophers, standard encyclopedic authors such as Pliny, Bede, and Isidore, and the author of the Hermetic *Asclepius*.[37] Furthermore, as Stock points out, Bernardus himself produces a commentary on his own myth: "In the course of telling the story of creation, he explains what creation is all about."[38]

The universe that is fashioned in the first book of the *Cosmographia* resembles, in essentials, at least, that of the other works I have been discussing. What is different is an emphasis on the sheer physical abundance of nature that makes the *Cosmographia* a joyous hymn to the splendors of the natural world. Indeed, the heroine of the work is Nature herself, the embodiment of the resurgent naturalism of the age. Some sense of this love for the physical may be gained simply from the summary of the first book—the *Megacosmus*, or "Greater Universe"—which precedes the narrative proper:

> Nature, as if in tears, makes complaint to Noys, or Divine Providence, about the confused state of primal matter, or Hyle, and pleads that the universe be more beautifully wrought. Noys, moved by her prayers, assents willingly to her appeal, and straightway separates the four elements from one another. She sets the nine hierarchies of angels in the heavens; fixes the stars in the firmament; arranges the signs of the Zodiac and sets the seven planetary orbs in motion beneath them; sets the four cardinal winds in mutual opposition. Then follow the creation of living creatures and an account of the position of earth at the center of things. Then

famous mountains are described, followed by the characteristics of animal life. Next are the famous rivers, followed by the characteristics of trees. Then the varieties of scents and spices are described. Next the kinds of vegetables, the characteristics of grains, and then the powers of herbs. Then the kinds of swimming creatures, followed by the race of birds. Then the source of life in animate creatures is discussed. Thus in the first book is described the ordered disposition of the elements.[39]

Yet this summary can hardly convey the poetic richness of Bernardus' catalogs of trees, birds, herbs and spices, rivers and mountains, in which each species receives its peculiar characterization, where we discover the "Carian fig, creased with wrinkles, that fig which was Adam's food," "the owl, whom the sun's kindly light makes blind," and the carp, "which lends distinction to the Loire."[40]

From even this brief glimpse at Bernardus' concerns, we can see how widely he differs from the earlier authors. His is a universe that catalogues reality, not ideas. Though as full as Martianus' hall of memory, its substance is the wealth of natural, created things, not the artifacts of fancy. Scipio's world, where the vastness of space diminishes the earth and mortal concerns, and where ethics are determined by the otherworldly goal of the stars, is stark and bare by comparison. And the visionary force of Plato's image of the universe in the Myth of Er, that distanced contemplation of the souls in the country of the dead, is transformed here by a profound sense of the unity of physical and spiritual reality. For although the soul, in the best Platonic fashion, finds its earthly habitation a place of temporary confinement, nonetheless "a single bond of love links unlike natures, though the flesh be of earth and the mind ethereal."[41]

Moreover, the universe itself is forged and maintained by what can only be called an erotic copula. As Peter Dronke points out, "Bernardus Silvestris's distinctive contribution to the idea of cosmic love was to transform it . . . into an idea of cosmic fertility, emphasizing the sexual and creative aspects of the universal ordering force in a way that none of his predecessors had done."[42] Thus at the end of the *Megacosmus*, we find that the production of living beings results from a chain of emanations from God that are impregnations as well: "For as Noys is forever pregnant of the divine will, she in turn informs Endelechia [that is, the World-Soul] with the images she conceives of the eternal patterns, Endelechia impresses them upon Nature, and Nature imparts to Imarmene [the principle of temporal continuity] what the well-being of the universe demands."[43] This copulative sequence gives a directness, an immediacy, to creation. Plato and others used the analogy of a seal imprinting figures on wax to explain the production of many beings from a single exemplar; Bernardus, however, combines this idea with the image of seed to transform an abstract notion of the "multiplication of species" into a concrete metaphor of sowing and fertilization. No better way could be devised for representing the principle of universal creation in a work whose chief protagonist is Nature herself.

Bernardus' book is an example of a specific allegorical form derived from Macrobius' injunctions in his *Commentary on the Dream of Scipio*. Under the name *integumentum* or *involucrum*, it is defined in a twelfth-century commentary on Virgil's *Aeneid* (attributed to Bernardus himself) as "the type of demonstration which wraps the thing comprehended under a fabulous narration of truth and is thus said to be an *involucrum* or envelope."[44] A similar definition appears in another commentary that has been assigned to Bernardus—this one on Martianus' *Marriage*.[45] Whether or not he is the author of these works is of secondary importance; what matters is that he wrote at a time when Macrobius' ideas on fabulous narrative not only were well known, but even served as a basis for contemporary literary theory.

When Bernardus creates an allegorical epic whose characters include such figures as Nature, Primal Matter, and the World-Soul, he acts in perfect conformity to Macrobius' proscriptions. This is the proper subject matter of fabulous narrative, for "just as [Nature] has removed an understanding of herself from the ordinary senses of men by a varied cloaking and concealment of her activities, so she has willed that her mysteries should be treated of by thoughtful men through myth."[46] Yet Bernardus, as we may have noted already, does not restrict himself to these limits. Noys, the Divine Providence, plays an even more significant role in the work than does Nature herself, and though her exact character remains ambiguous, one of the functions she incorporates is that of the *Nous,* the Divine Mind of Neoplatonism.[47] She even describes herself as "the consummate and profound reason of God, whom his prime substance brought forth of itself, a second self, . . . the knowledge and judgment of the divine will in the disposition of things."[48] Likewise the Mirror of Providence, which Noys gives to Urania to help her create a soul for man, is itself "the eternal mind, in which resides that unfathomable understanding, that intellect which is the creator and the destroyer of all things."[49] Vast in size, it contains an indelible array of the exemplars or Platonic forms of all things that will ever come into existence.

Bernardus, then, has knowingly violated Macrobius' rule against fabulous treatment of "that Mind, which the Greeks call *Nous,* containing the original concepts of things, the *ideai,* that Mind born of and proceeding from the supreme God."[50] Yet he goes further still, for the chief proscription is against the use of fabulous narrative to discuss God himself, "called by the Greeks the good *(tagathon)* and the First Cause *(proton aition).*"[51] (The terms appear in the manuscripts of the *Commentary* in Greek, often in a somewhat garbled form.) In the fifth chapter of the *Microcosmus,* however, as Urania and Nature, having journeyed through the heavens, reach the limits of the universe, they come upon "the secret abode of the supreme and super-essential God."[52] This is a supernally brilliant place inhabited by the supreme deity, otherwise known as *Tugaton:*

> From that realm . . . a radiant splendor shines forth, nowhere partial, but everywhere infinite and eternal. This inaccessible brilliance so strikes the eyes of the beholder, so confounds his vision, that since the radiance shields itself by its very radiance, you may perceive that the splendor produces of itself an obscuring darkness.[53]

Here, by an adroit manipulation of the mystical terminology of Pseudo-Dionysius, for whom God is "dazzling darkness,"[54] Bernardus creates a heavenly artifact that exists on the narrow borderline between the fabulous image and pure analogy.

Bernardus is walking a thin edge here, rather as Martianus did in an earlier age. The supreme divinity is an important constituent of his world scheme, and he cannot forbear bringing him into his tale. But he can and does forbear to confine him in an image. Tugaton, "the Good," remains outside the world, disembodied and reflected only through his gleaming domicile, itself a mystically paradoxical composite. It operates upon the world by a hierarchical mediation of energy, that first brilliant streaming by which it makes itself known being distributed to the lower realms of creation through the varied orders of angels and other spiritual beings. Bernardus' universe is, in effect, a Christianized version of Martianus's. As full and as varied, it achieves a more pleasing and harmonious tone by the superposition of Christian angelology upon Martianus's eclectic system of gods and spirits and by the ordering principle of cosmic love that rules its motions.

Since Bernardus is not bound by a commitment to the sacred status of the *Nous,* he is afforded a versatile protagonist for his tale; yet, since his theology demands the transcendence of the supreme being, his treatment of God remains within the limits set by Macrobius. In the *Cosmographia* we find a solution to the problems of Neoplatonic allegory that will not be bettered in the Middle Ages. Later in the twelfth century, Alan of Lille, who has Martianus and Bernardus for models, adopts the figure of Noys in his *Anticlaudianus,* but her role there is only a minor one. Like Philology, Phronesis, the heroine of Alan's epic, finds God at the end of her celestial voyage. Yet, though he has kept his splendor, he has lost his mystery: portrayed as the King of the heavens, he speaks and has a form that we can comprehend. Dante's *Divine Comedy,* the culmination of this tradition, restores some of the power and mystery of God's incomprehensibility. After having seen the spiritual wonders of Heaven, Dante, in the last lines of the *Paradiso,* has a vision of the Trinity. Three gleaming circles appear in an aureole; they reflect one another, and upon one there emerges the figure of a man. This is the mystery that he cannot fathom, upon which his "high imagination" runs aground, leaving him devoid of will and open to the force of universal love. Like Bernardus he has seen the point where the image fails, where all images must fail, and even the form of God as man cannot wholly satisfy the mind.

Although the works that I have been discussing may seem the products of an age whose concerns have little to do with ours and whose ideas about the constitution of the universe and man's place in it are foreign to our own, there are a number of reasons why they should be of more than mere historical interest to us. Not only do they reflect the mind of the poet and of the philosopher at work using and reshaping the cosmos to provide the expressive setting for his thoughts; they also comprise a tradition of speculative fiction that does not simply come to an end with the Renaissance or with the scientific revolution, but continues to have representatives into our own time. C. S. Lewis is, of course, the most obvious example. He is steeped in all these works, and a book such as *Out of the Silent Planet* derives not only incidental elements of plot, but also important themes and perhaps even its overall narrative form from them. It may, in fact, not be too much to say that the tradition of philosophical fable that begins with the Myth of Er is a major precursor to modern science fiction, especially that which leans toward allegory. To see this current of speculation as viable today—and to consider writers such as Lindsay and Lewis science fiction writers—is to posit an alternate mode of world-making fiction. It is one that not only resists Suvin's foreshortening process, which would overlap the here and the elsewhere, but also reshapes the empirical world to conform, not to some dynamic, inexorable process, but to a fixed vision or idea. Thus what we might call Platonic science fiction has been a powerful force in the Western literary tradition that has both shaped at least one of the great works of world literature, the *Divine Comedy,* and, in a larger sense, opened a field for the visionary imagination that is still fertile today.

Dialogues Concerning Human Understanding: Empirical Views of God from Locke to Lem

Stephen W. Potts

Science fiction, as a genre, has traditionally supplied its readers with plenty of confrontations with the unknown; indeed, there would be little to science fiction without them. Like science itself, however, science fiction has also traditionally had a low tolerance for that which remains unknown. Most readers of science fiction expect, and receive, answers to all questions raised; most science fiction, true to its roots in scientific empiricism, presents the triumph of human reason over the irrational, the alien, the mysterious, the initially mind-boggling. To treat of the unknowable, to raise more questions than one can answer, has been the conventional territory of the philosophical and literary mainstream. Yet even general relativity is in part an admission of the limitations of human knowledge. As cosmologists strain to translate the story the quasar tells and as physicists seek the ultimate order of all things in the elusive subnuclear realm of the quark, an old question resurrects: Is there a limit to what human reason can known and do? Can man understand the nature and purpose of the cosmos, or through reason achieve unity with what has historically been known as God?

Stanislaw Lem deals with these very questions in a number of his works, the best known of which is *Solaris*. The ostensible plot of *Solaris* concerns a small group of men on a scientific station orbiting the planet Solaris, which is covered, inhabited one could say, by an organic "ocean" that regularly manifests indications of intelligence and self-direction, the most recent of which, and the one that motivates the plot, is its incarnating in humanoid form the subconscious guilts of those on the station. In the case of the narrator, Kris Kelvin, that means the unshakable presence of his young wife, Rheya, who killed herself years before as a result of Kelvin's withdrawing love from her. But this plot is in fact only a metaphor for the theme of the work, which weaves overtly in and out of the chapters.

At three points in the course of events, the narrator seeks answers—or refuge—in the station library, where he explores the tomes that record the century-long history of Solaristics. What unfolds is a pathetic account of humanity's endeavor to understand the utterly alien life form of the planet, of man's struggle to achieve that consummate cosmic goal—Contact. But the Crusade is frustrated time and time again; new theories of the ocean's nature and behavior give way to new disillusionments when they prove false, and humankind's attitude toward Solaris and Solaristics gradually evolves from empirical curiosity to mystified reverence to cynical despair. There remains little question that the endeavor is doomed, hopeless. Lem also leaves little doubt as to why.

The first broad clue appears in a conversation between Kelvin and the Solarist Dr. Snow, when the latter is informing Kelvin about the subconscious origins of the visitors sent by the ocean. Dr. Snow is old, a longtime resident of the station, driven to cynicism and alcohol by the latest turn of events and by the overall failure of Solaristics to accomplish its original goal. As he tells Kelvin, "We don't want to conquer the cosmos; we simply want to extend the boundaries of the Earth to the frontiers of the cosmos. . . . We think of ourselves as the Knights of the Holy Contact. This is another lie. We are only seeking Man. We have no need of other worlds. We need mirrors."[1]

However, it is throughout the various histories and texts that Kelvin studies that the reasons for humanity's inability to understand the ocean—to achieve Contact—are most explicitly set forth. Man insists on viewing the ocean with the reflective lens of anthropomorphism. During his researches Kelvin refers to "our compulsion to superimpose analogies with what we know" and to "giving way to the temptations of a latent anthropomorphism" in describing the ocean's behavior. At one point, after reviewing in one text several attempts of scientists to comprehend the complex abstractions constantly created from the ocean's surface in terms of terrestrial forms, he notes, "There was no escaping the impressions that grew out of man's experience on earth. The prospects of Contact receded."[2]

These conclusions are underlined and elaborated upon in a pamphlet Kelvin later comes across, the work of one eccentric autodidact named Grastrom, who asserts that all of humanity's most abstract achievements in science, such as the theory of relativity, have been no more than projections of our own physiological limitations. Therefore, man could never truly understand anything in the cosmos beyond himself, and "there neither was, nor could be, any question of 'contact' between mankind and any nonhuman civilization."[3] Yet, despite the growing awareness of Solarists and of the human species in general that the hopes of eventual Contact are fruitless, despite the metaphysical pain that results from that knowledge, the endeavor to understand the ocean of Solaris doggedly, if much less enthusiastically, continues.

Contact, in fact, is less a scientific than a religious goal. One of the more cynical Solarists that Kelvin reads and explains to us is Muntius, who describes Solaristics as "the space era's equivalent of religion" or "faith described as science." As evidence, he points to a number of parallels between the two—the refusal of Solarists to acknowledge arguments that undermine the foundations of their belief, the effort to discover in the ocean some body of ultimate meaning that is by its nature untranslatable into human terms and thus incommunicable. In Kelvin's paraphrase, "unconsciously it is Revelation itself that they expect, and this revelation is to explain to them the meaning of the destiny of man! Solaristics is a revival of long-vanished myths, the expression of mystical nostalgias which men are unwilling to confess openly. The cornerstone is deeply entrenched in the foundations of the edifice: it is the hope of Redemption."[4]

Originally, Kelvin notes, still paraphrasing Muntius, Contact, which Solarists had always avoided defining, was to be a beginning. Over the years it had become an end in itself—"the Mission of Mankind." The tragedy of Solaristics, and the theme of the novel, is that though everyone loves a mystery human nature cannot bear one that insists on remaining a mystery.

A similar theme threads through another of Lem's novels. In *The Investigation*, Scotland Yard is given the task of explaining the apparent resurrections of a number of corpses in a particular region of the English countryside. The inspectors assume, logically, that a human perpetrator is behind the disappearances of the bodies and then attempt, through logic, to make the empirical facts fit their conclusion. Even when it seems clear that no human being could have committed the alleged crimes, the obvious supernatural conclusion remains impossible to accept. Refusing to believe in miracles, the protagonist, Inspector Gregory, goes so far as to assign the behavior of the corpses to an intelligent microbe, "a microbe with the ability to think ahead the way a human being does."[5] Finally, Gregory conspires with his superior to explain away the "crimes" as the work of a truck driver who had, conveniently, died in an accident shortly after the incidents ceased. In other words, if the facts do not permit an anthropocentric conclusion, create one.

No image better sums up the novel's theme than that in which Gregory, wandering through London in search of explanations, stumbles into a shopping arcade where he confronts a dark figure that will not let him pass. On the verge of violence, he suddenly realizes he is facing a mirror in a deadend; the figure is his own reflection. Ultimately, all Man can know is Man.

It should be clear that the questions raised by the investigation, as by the failure of Solaristics, go much beyond the novels themselves. Indeed, these questions—the limitations of human reason and its capability to comprehend God, the supernatural, the Absolute—have preoccupied metaphysicians and theologians in one form or another since the Hellenic dawn of Western philosophy and with specific reference to empiricism since the beginning of the scientific age in the seventeenth century. In fact, in these works, and in *Solaris* in particular, Lem adds another chapter to a dialogue that finds its source among such philosophers as Locke and Hume and that comes to us after centuries of alternating belief, skepticism, paradox, and dispute.

In his afterword to the Berkley edition of *Solaris*, Darko Suvin provides the reader with a helpful overview of Lem's philosophical roots and suggests his interest in seventeenth- and eighteenth-century thought. It is no coincidence that during those centuries empirical materialism first flourished, challenging the long-accepted faiths of Christian idealism.

The empiricists themselves resisted identification with skepticism and atheism, attempting to prove through their new rationalism the existence of God and the inherent presence of a recognizable moral order in the universe. In *An Essay Concerning Humane Understanding,* John Locke argued that knowledge depended on the evidence of the senses, on the impressions of solid facts and observations on the human mind. Like his immediate predecessor Descartes, however, he bent his thesis somewhat in order to prove the existence of the Deity. Locke asserted: "To show, therefore, that we are capable of *knowing,* i.e., being certain that there is a God, and *how we may come by* this certainty, I think we need go no further than *ourselves,* and that undoubted knowledge of our own existence."[6] He offered as proof that man and creation could not exist—and the evidence of our senses manifestly demonstrates that these do exist—without a preexisting Absolute, since to imagine something created from nothing is absurd; and this preexisting something has to be a reasoning being because man is a reasoning being and could not have been created by matter insensate. Locke, therefore, using his empirical method, managed to create God once again in man's image, utilizing the impressions that have grown out of man's experience on Earth.

Less than a century later, David Hume carried the discussion forward in his *Dialogues Concerning Natural Religion*. In this work the spokesman for empiricism, who ultimately receives the narrator's stamp of approval, defends himself against two disputants, one a Platonic idealist left over from the earlier Age of Faith and the other a skeptic doubting the capabilities of human reason. The empirical position as stated here is that the order of the universe can be inferred from the order of the human mind, that the laws by which the cosmos operates are much the same as those one can observe in operation on earth, and that the characteristics of the Deity are evident in the highest ideals and noblest qualities of man. The idealist argues that God and the cosmos are beyond the ken of mere mortals, since human understanding is earthbound and therefore flawed. The reply of the skeptic to the empiricist is even more pointed. After insisting that man and all he knows on earth is only one tiny portion of the universe and not the model for the whole of it, he inquires, "Why select so minute, so weak, so bounded a principle as the reason and design of animals is found to be on his planet? What peculiar privilege has this little agitation of the brain which we call *thought*, that we must thus make it the model of the whole universe?" And he asks, "Is there any reasonable ground to conclude, that the inhabitants of other planets possess thought, intelligence, reason, or anything similar to these faculties in men?" and later, with reference to God, "And will any man tell me with a serious countenance, that an orderly universe must arise from some thought or art, like the human; because we have experience of it?"[7]

Throughout the *Dialogues* the skeptic and the idealist are frequently able to agree on the remoteness and incomprehensibility of God. In the opinion of both, the major philosophical sin of the empiricist is his anthropomorphic view of God and the universe. Even though, with many reservations, the skeptic ultimately concedes "that the cause or causes of order in the universe probably bear some remote analogy to human intelligence," he still maintains that his empirical opponent is an "anthropomorphite."[8] The skeptic argues his point well, and the charge seems to stick. Even the narrator must accord some wisdom to the skeptic's position when the dialogue ends. Yet, as we all know, empirical materialism, anthropocentric though it was, eventually triumphed, making our age of science possible while carrying its anthropocentrism with it.

Platonic idealism, which had retired in defeat from Hume's work, nevertheless had not given up the struggle. A century after the *Dialogues,* it went on the offensive again in the metaphysics of Søren Kierkegaard, whose *Fear and Trembling* explored the limitations of human understanding in confronting the mysteries of the divine. Written in part as a reply to two Hegelian materialists of his own day, *Fear and Trembling* is built around the Old Testament tale in which God, to test the faith of the patriarch Abraham, commands him to sacrifice his son Isaac. Kierkegaard repeatedly points out that by any human ethical standard God's request is outrageous, wholly offensive to any concepts of right and good, and that Abraham, in demonstrating his willingness to obey, shows himself by human standards an infanticide and an immoral beast. But he makes clear that human standards are not divine standards and that, in exercising his faith despite the horrified awareness of what he is doing, Abraham proves himself the holiest of men. Because of the absolute nature of the Deity, an absoluteness implicit by definition in the concept of deity, human understanding can only fall hopelessly short; the more the human mind attempts to comprehend the ultra-Platonic divine will through rational means, the further it will find itself enmeshed in paradox, since the Absolute is not accessible to human reason. Thus, Kierkegaard concludes, man, if he wishes to be one with the meaning and purpose of the universe, must embrace the irrational, the paradoxical, the *absurd;* he must take a "leap of faith" over and beyond reason.

If this leap was difficult for thinkers in Kierkegaard's time—a fact manifested as well in the work of Melville and of Dostoevsky—it had become virtually impossible by the beginning of the twentieth century. Nowhere is the resultant metaphysical *angst* better expressed than in the morose, complex work of Franz Kafka. An avid reader of Kierkegaard, Kafka pursued theological paradox in his parables and longer fiction. While much controversy continues to permeate Kafka criticism, there remains little doubt that the religious content of Kafka's work, if not the sole aspect of it, is at least an important one. Some have gone so far as to see in Kafka's two major novels, *The Trial* and *The Castle,* the individual's pursuit of, respectively, divine justice and divine grace. The already complicated works are made even more problematic by the fact that neither was finished. Kafka's parables, however, may provide some clue to the meanings of these novels.

One central concern is best demonstrated by the parable *Vor dem Gesetz,* translatable as "Before the Law" or "Before the Court," which appears near the climax of *The Trial.* It relates the history of a man who comes to the gateway of absolute authority only to find his ingress blocked by a stern and sturdy gatekeeper. The man tries to reason with the guard, but repeatedly fails to get permission to pass. He cannot overpower the guard, who warns that, even if the man could, there are many gates beyond, each with a mightier gatekeeper than the last. The man, wanting nothing but to enter the Court of the Law, spends his lifetime alongside the gate, unable to persuade the gatekeeper or even the fleas in his fur collar. The gatekeeper himself becomes the sole object of the man's attentions, and all beyond the gate is forgotten. At his death the man is told by the guard that this entrance was meant only for him, and with that the guard closes it.

Of similar import is the parable "An Imperial Message," in which the Emperor, the bright Imperial sun, has sent a message to the reader, the most microscopic of his subjects, from his deathbed. The message, of singular, even divine, importance, is whispered into the ear of his strongest and most trusted messenger, who makes his way through the crowd that jams the Emperor's chamber. But after forcing his way through one crowd, he has to confront a crowd in the next chamber, and another in the one after that. And even if he can get through the chambers of the innermost palace, he still has to fight his way through stairways and courtyards, then still another palace. And if after thousands of years he has managed the impossible and arrived at the outermost gate, he still has the overflowing throngs of the capital city to push through. The message can never reach its destination across so many insurmountable barriers.

In both parables the goal—ultimate understanding, presumably of the cosmos—is frustrated by the presence of man-made or manlike barriers, gates and gatekeeepers, walls and courtyards. In the novels these serial obstacles are created by bureaucracies of infinite complexity, consisting of layer upon layer of officials, clerks, messengers, servants, and other human operatives; in each the protagonist barely gets beyond the first obstruction before his strength gives out or he is defeated. In both parables the walls, the gates, and the bureaucracies established to protect the Truth finally prevent anyone from reaching it. Unable to comprehend the cosmos, yet unable to abandon that quest, man reaches an impass; his striving for redemption degenerates into a hopeless struggle with a single human obstacle—a stubborn guard or an apathetic clerk.

One of the strongest arguments posed in opposition to the religious interpretation of Kafka's novels is that the institutions supposedly embodying divine law and acceptance are disgustingly corrupt, venal, and all too fallibly human. The metaphysical critics, in reply, have fallen back on Kierkegaard, pointing up the ethical distinctions he makes between the unknowable laws by which the Deity operates and the moral laws of man. But it is more likely that Kafka's bureaucracies, mistaken by humanity for the Absolute, are in fact merely human constructs, paradigms of man's reason.

Unfortunately, in recreating the universe in his own image and in modeling the Truth on the machinations of his own mind, man has unwittingly sacrificed his ability to make Kierkegaard's "leap of faith." Unable to transcend empirical anthropocentrism, man is left with unfulfilled hopes and the endless, doomed continuation of the search. For—and herein lies the source of much of Kafka's *angst*—the hope and the search continue, *must* continue, though they become ends in themselves and lead ultimately to despair, defeat, and death.

Kafka remains a part of the literary soil of Eastern Europe; in Poland he is, in fact, now celebrated as a master of the absurd.[9] A number of scholars have noted his influence on Lem,[10] particularly in regard to *Memoirs Found in a Bathtub,* which depicts a man struggling through a multilayered bureaucracy called "the Building" in pursuit of his Mission, primarily trying to discover what it is. Official after official thwarts the agent; clerk after clerk delays him. He stumbles from level to level, room to room, every step leading him further from the goal of ultimate comprehension, of understanding his role in the order of things—or the order of things itself. Certain scenes and images come directly out of Kafka. For instance, when one secretary refuses him immediate entry to an important official, the narrator must wait in the outer office. Following repeated subsequent refusals, he commences pleading with her, plying her with questions and confessions, at one point screaming into her indifferent ear. Eventually, he has no choice but to give up and go elsewhere. This secretary is by no means the only gatekeeper in the novel; indeed, one character is even called Gatekeeper. Yet at the end, despite the agent's repeated failures, despite everything he suffers, he discovers that "against, entirely against, my better knowledge—I still held on to my faith—like a last hope, a hope against hope—in that accursed, that thrice accursed Mission of

mine.''[11] Though defeated by the indecipherable snarl of contradictions and paradoxes, by the flawed constructs of humankind's pre-
tentious rationality, he finds himself unable to discontinue his search
for purpose.

Attempting to achieve redemption, to comprehend the ultimate
purpose and meaning of the universe, Lem's Solarists have met the
same fate as the seeker in *Memoirs Found in a Bathtub* and for the
same reason: the imperfect nature of human reason. Yet, in the
closing chapter of *Solaris,* Kelvin perhaps finds a solution to this
problem. With Rheya and the other visitors finally gone, Kelvin
engages in philosophical discussion with the weary Snow. They consider the possibility that the ocean may be an imperfect god, a
supernatural child just learning to handle its power. Darko Suvin
takes the suggestion seriously; David Ketterer observes that it is
probably just one more anthropomorphic theory.[12] Kelvin insists,
however, that his imperfect god is neither the ocean nor another
reflection of man; it is, instead, ''the only god I could imagine believing in, a god whose passion is not a redemption, who saves nothing,
fulfills no purpose—a god who simply is.''[13]

To understand the nature of this god as Lem intends it to be
understood, one must turn—as with Kafka—to one of the author's
shorter parables. In ''The Twenty-First Voyage'' of Ijon Tichy in
Lem's *Star Diaries,* the planet-hopping protagonist comes upon a
community of robot friars living in catacombs under a world in
which all logical support for belief has been made impossible by the
infinite possibilities of science. For centuries this planet's humanity,
like our own empiricists, had endeavored ''to accumulate arguments
and proofs for God's existence and, when those inevitably crumble,
to take the bits and chips and raise them up anew.''[14] But the more
empirical knowledge and material power one accumulates, as the
mechanical prior points out, the further away God becomes. Reason
and faith are irreconcilable, and the former cannot be used to
strengthen the latter.

The robots believe simply because ''belief is the only thing that
cannot be taken from a conscious entity, so long as that entity consciously cleaves to it.'' Their faith is ''completely naked . . . and
completely defenseless.'' According to the prior, ''We entertain no
hopes, make no demands, requests, we count on nothing, we only
believe.''[15] And a passage of striking significance follows:

> If someone believes for certain reasons and on certain
> grounds, his faith loses its full sovereignty; that two and two

are four I know right well and therefore need not have faith in it. But of God I know nothing, and therefore can *only* have faith. What does this faith give me? By the ancient reckoning, not a blessed thing. No longer is it the anodyne for the dread of extinction, no longer the heavenly courtier lobbying for salvation and against damnation. It does not allay the mind, tormented by the contradictions of existence; it does not smooth out those edges; I tell you—it is worthless! Which means it serves no end. We cannot even declare that *this* is the reason we believe, because such faith reduces to absurdity: he who would speak thus is in effect claiming to know the difference—permanently—between the absurd and the not absurd, and has himself chosen the absurd because, according to him, that is the side on which God stands. We do not argue this. Our act of faith is neither supplicating nor thankful, neither humble nor defiant, it simply *is,* and there is nothing more that can be said about it.[16]

The faith of the robot friars pointedly counters empiricism's anthropocentric dependence on logic and reason and the Kierkegaardian idealist's pridefully humble surrender to the absurd.

Following his experience with Solaris, and shortly before declaring his possible belief in this god, Kelvin asserts: "I shall never again give myself completely to anything or anybody. . . . I shall remember my follies and my hopes. And this future Kelvin will be no less worthy a man than the Kelvin of the past, who was prepared for anything in the name of an ambitious enterprise called Contact. Nor will any man have the right to judge me."[17] Like the friars, Kelvin has not necessarily renounced empiricism, but he has renounced mankind's foolish endeavor to comprehend rationally the nonhuman with human models. He has at the same time renounced the idealist's absolute god of judgment and redemption. In so doing he has avoided the despair that Kafka perceived in the unbridgeable gap between man and the Absolute; he has turned his back on the ultimate transcendence that Kierkegaard saw in God and that the Solarists saw in Contact. In fact, Kelvin much resembles Hume's skeptic, who also argues convincingly for the necessity for an imperfect God, an agnostic's God, the god of the robot friars. Having broken the tenuous link between scientific empiricism and mankind's yearning for redemption, Kelvin has cleared the way for a new kind of commitment, an open-ended commitment.

After his dialogue with Snow, Kelvin descends to the planet to meet the ocean on its own territory. Arriving on the shore of an old mimoid—a floating scab of an island—Kelvin reaches out toward an oily, organic wave. It envelops his hand without touching him—contact, but not quite. After Kelvin tries the same experiment with the same results a few times, the ocean grows indifferent and avoids his still-extended hand. Although he had read several accounts of this phenomenon, he says, "none of them had prepared me for the experience as I had lived it, and I felt somehow changed. . . . I had never felt the ocean's gigantic presence so strongly, or its powerful changeless silence, or the secret forces that gave the waves their regular rise and fall. I sat unseeing, and sank into a universe of inertia, glided down an irresistible slope and identified myself with the dumb, fluid colossus; it was as if I had forgiven it everything, without the slightest effort of word or thought."[18]

Having lost Rheya, his own single anthropomorphic link with the ocean, he asks himself why he should stay, probing the ocean, seeking the purpose it appears to have. "I hoped for nothing," he says. "And yet I lived in expectation. Since she was gone, that was all that remained. . . . I knew nothing, and I persisted in the faith that the time of cruel miracles was not past."[19] His unseeing, unreasoning identification with the ocean certainly seems like a Kierkegaardian leap of faith. But, if indeed a leap into the irrational, it is an existential leap, not in pursuit of God or the Absolute, but with a mind wholly open to all experience, with no judgments or anthropocentric conclusions preordained. Like Kafka's protagonists, Kelvin preserves his sense of expectation while understanding nothing; unlike them, but like the friars of Ijon Tichy's "Twenty-First Voyage," he hopes for nothing either. Ironically, at this point he has become the logical extrapolation of the earlier empiricism, an empty slate ready to receive the universe on its own terms, to accept—to quote the friars—"existence in its entirety," a conclusion implied long ago in the well-argued stance of the skeptic in Hume's *Dialogues.* It would not be unlike Lem's active wit to have hinted at this eventuallity in a pun; like the scale of temperature that bears his name, Kelvin now begins at absolute zero.

In *Solaris,* in *The Investigation,* and more pointedly in "The Twenty-First Voyage" of Ijon Tichy, Stanislaw Lem deals directly with the issues raised by Locke, Hume, and Kierkegaard, and in terms that could only come out of a familiarity with the work and thought of these philosophers. Lem not only extrapolates—in the honored fashion of science fiction writers—from scientific theory; he calls into question the entire set of assumptions underlying any naïvely positivistic thought. To accept without question the empirical principles that inform our age—as so many readers and writers of science fiction have done—is to commit the sin of Solaristics and to create the universe in the image of earth, to see in the multifarious faces of God no more than a reflection of ourselves. In going deeper into Western tradition than many modern science fiction writers are willing to go, Lem unearths a richer vein of material and, pursuant to the law of geological succession, one with sources further back in time. Lem's work reminds us that, after all, our scientific tradition grows out of our philosophical tradition.

Aliens and Knowability:
A Scientist's Perspective

Gregory Benford

J. G. Ballard has said that one of the problems of science fiction is that it is not a literature won from experience. There are several ways of interpreting this assertion. It is nowhere more obviously true, though, than in the case of science fiction that depicts aliens.

I shall discuss some of the philosophical and literary problems of treating aliens. My discussion will probably not resemble most literary criticism because I am not a critic, but a science fiction writer and a physicist. And I do not pretend to objectivity or even to impartiality, since I have written some fiction about this subject and am therefore already biased. I shall attempt a brief catalog of the ways aliens have been depicted in science fiction and then move on to the philosophical problems that interest me. I shall necessarily give only slight attention to many rich areas.

Anthropocentric Aliens

By far the most common kind of alien in science fiction is the unexamined one—supposedly strange, but represented by only a few aspects, all of which are merely exaggerations of human traits. The simplest version of this kind of alien is the invader, often depicted as an implacable, mindless threat (as in Robert Heinlein's *Puppet Masters* and *Starship Troopers*). In making easy political analogies, the film *The Thing* is fairly typical of a vast body of science fiction: the Thing stands for the Communist menace, the wooly-minded scientists who try to make contact with it despite its obvious hostility represent the Adlai Stevensons of this world, and the United States Air Force stands for, of course, the United States

53

Air Force. A more interesting version of the anthropomorphic alien is typified by Hal Clement's Mesklinites in *Mission of Gravity*. They have unusual bodies, determined by their bizarre planetary surroundings. This "biology as destiny" theme occurs often in science fiction, but, like the Mesklinites, the aliens of such stories commonly speak like Midwesterners of the 1950s and are otherwise templates of stock humans. In Larry Niven's *Ringworld,* variants on this kind of alien are represented by beings roughly equivalent to types of terrestrial animals. Niven's kzinti is a catlike carnivore, given to mindless rages. His puppeteers are herd animals (that is, cowards); their cities stink, like a corral. In *People of the Wind,* Poul Anderson has done this sort of thing with more subtlety, giving his bird aliens touches of real strangeness.

In my view, the trouble with most realizations of this much-sought strangeness is that its effect so soon wears off. Larry Niven and Jerry Pournelle's *Mote in God's Eye* explores aliens who are not bilaterally symmetric (an odd variant, indeed) and extracts some value from the feel of threeness versus twoness. In the end, though, these aliens seem no more difficult to understand than the Chinese. (Indeed, there is an uncomfortable resemblance in the old Space Navy method of dealing with them.) They are stopped from spreading by a technicality involving faster-than-light travel; this insures that alien values and threenesses do not flood through the sevagram.

Even as respected a work as Olaf Stapledon's *Star Maker* does not truly focus on the alienness of the many creatures that inhabit its future worlds. Stapledon gives them biological variations that ultimately have no impact whatever on the gross socioeconomic forces at work in the environment around them. There are no alternate realities here, no genuinely different ways of looking at the universe, but instead (on the planetary level, at least) a clockwork Marxism that drives them inevitably into tired confrontations of labor with capital, and so on. It is the larger vision Stapledon pursued, his account of the ultimate grinding down of the galaxies, that still moves us today. The Marxism is the most dated aspect of his work.

A related function of aliens in science fiction is that of a mirror (or foil). The sexual strangeness of the Gethenians in Ursula Le Guin's *Left Hand of Darkness,* for example, is a distancing device, a way to examine our own problems in a different light. In countless lesser works aliens are really stand-in humans of the Zenna Henderson sort: quasi-human, with emotions and motivations not much different from our own. Aliens as mirrors for our own experiences abound in science fiction. Arthur C. Clarke's "Rescue Party" has humans as its true focus, though the action centers on aliens who are only a dumber version of ourselves. The final lines of the story give us a human-chauvinist thrill, telling us more about ourselves than we nowadays wish to know.

The Galactic Empire motif, with its equations of planet=colony and aliens=Indians (of either variety), is a common, unimaginative indulgence of science fiction. There are generally no true aliens in such epics, only a retreading of our own history. This underlying structure is so common in science fiction, even now, that it is difficult to know whether we should attribute it to simple lack of imagination or to a deep, unconscious need to return repeatedly to the problem. It would be interesting to see an Asian science fiction writer tackle the same theme. The list of aliens-as-foils is large. Authors have treated women as aliens, children as aliens, and robots as alienlike. In such tales we are really saying something about ourselves, not about the universe beyond us. An especially pointed use of this device was made by Brian Aldiss in *The Dark Light Years,* in which aliens use excrement as a sacrament. This stress on the holiness of returning to the soil so that the cycle of life may go on mirrors some Eastern ideas, though its main target may be Western scatology.

I end this catalog of more conventional uses of aliens by bringing up a puzzle I think worth pondering. It has long been clear (to any biologist who has thought about the question for more than five minutes) that any alien planetary ecology will be utterly different from ours. The old cliché—open the helmet, sniff the air: "Smells good! We can breathe it"—is usually avoided these days, but more subtle technical difficulties are not. Even if, for example, we found alien plants we could stomach, anything they contained resembling sugar could easily have the wrong sense of rotation from Earthly ones and thus would be unusable as food. Proteins, trace minerals—all would almost certainly be incompatible with our organic systems. To make a planet habitable by humans, we would have to erase what is there and introduce an entirely new, man-oriented ecology. Yet, in thousands of otherwise respectable science fiction stories, this point is ignored. Why? If questioned, most science fiction authors would, I imagine, admit the point and plead the convenience of assuming otherwise. Yet this sidestepping of the problem is not simply a bit of insiders' footwork, as is, say, faster-than-light travel. When a new theoretical fillip for getting such high velocities appears, the hard–science fiction writers instantly snatch it up and ring some changes on it; I have done so myself. But we never really touch the ecology problem. Seldom do we admit in fiction that it *is* a problem. I can think of only two recent works that address the issue: Joanna Russ' *We Who Are About To.* . . . and Lloyd Biggle's *Monument*. The almost universal avoidance of this striking astronomical-biological fact must have some motivation. Is it a telltale signal of some deep fear? Does it indicate that we do not care to smudge the image of a difficult but generally sympathetic galaxy out there? I do not know. But I do think the problem is worth the attention of the critics.

Unknowable Aliens

For me, the most interesting aspect of the alien lies, not in its use as a fresh enemy, an analog human, or a mirror for ourselves, but rather in its essential strangeness. Remarkably few science fiction works have considered the alien at this most basic level. One which does is Arthur C. Clarke's *Rendezvous with Rama*. The vast space vehicle, Rama, yields up some of its secrets, but leaves our solar system with its essential nature shrouded. We see the mechanisms, but not the mind behind them. Since Ringworld and Rama there has been a tendency to use giganticism as an easy signifier of alienness, as in John Varley's *Titan* trilogy, but I feel the method yields diminishing returns. Size alone is not all that significant. Let us remember that some of the most bizarre aspects of reality appear at the subatomic level.

The biggest entity of all, of course, is God. Aliens often have a strong theological role, as in the metaphors of ascension in Clarke's *Childhood's End* and *2001: A Space Odyssey*. Aliens do occasionally appear in science fiction as distant, inexplicable things, often ignored by the human characters. Making them objects of indifference does not exploit or illuminate the philosophical problems involved, though. These emerge when other beings attempt communication with them.

One of the basic devices of science fiction is the instant translator, which enables aliens to speak an Earthly language with little difficulty (in science fiction, English, often American English, at that). This device serves to speed up a story, but writers using it sidestep a knotty problem: how can beings be strange and still communicate with us easily? Some authors have been able to surmount this difficulty, but few have used the language problem itself as a major turning point. The essence of epistemology is language, for only by communicating our perceptions can we get them checked. The intuitive bedrock of perception must be given voice. Ian Watson's *Embedding* involves aliens who come to barter with us for our languages (not our sciences or arts), for languages are the keys to a deeper knowledge. By assembling all the galaxy's tongues, they believe they will transcend their species limitations and at last understand the real world. Thus the language of each species is capable of rendering a partial picture.

In another visit by aliens to the Earth (depicted in *If the Stars Are Gods* by Gordon Eklund and me), the aliens seek communion with our star, not with us. Their picture of reality involves stars as spiritual entities. The protagonist at first believes the aliens are lying, but is later drawn into their world view. He sees their vision and reaches some sort of understanding. But the paradoxes that run through the text turn about at the end, and he sees himself as trapped, by his own use of human categories, into a fundamental ignorance of the aliens. A Wittgenstein quotation, ''A dog cannot be a hypocrite, but neither can he be sincere,'' underlines the limits of using human concepts. The emotional reaction to this view is also varied: the aliens are deliberately compared to pastel giraffes, and there are other comic touches. The layered paradoxes of the story line all suggest a possibility of ''communion with the suns,'' but also the impossibility of knowing whether this sense, as filtered by human minds, is what the aliens mean. Reflections of this basic either-or, subject-other habitual mind-set occur throughout this work, always pointing toward an irreducible strangeness.

The most extreme view one can take is to reject the notion of any degree of possible knowledge of the alien, to declare all the aliens of science fiction inherently anthropomorphic or anthropocentric, and to state flatly that true aliens would be fundamentally unknowable. This position is perhaps best put forward in Stanislaw Lem's *Solaris*. In *New Worlds for Old* David Ketterer has explored the many images and phrases Lem uses to underline his position. The library scene adroitly satirizes science as model building, for example. In his afterword to the novel, Darko Suvin attributes Lem's renunciation of final truths to ''the bitter experiences of Central European intellectuals in this century.''[1] If this were in fact the only reason to adopt such a position, *Solaris* would not be important, but of course the philosophical roots of these ideas go quite deep.

A Philosophical Digression

One might at first ascribe Lem's point of view to the failure of positivistic philosophy in this century. Philosophy has taken quite a few lumps from mathematics in this regard. (Recall that Kant held the truths of geometry to be synthetic *a priori*. Relativity and Riemann came along shortly thereafter, and now even little children in the streets of Göttingen know that geometry is in fact a synthetic *a posteriori* category, a checkable fact. And we do not live in a Euclidean universe, either, as Kant imagined.) The thrust of mathematical philosophy has been toward arithmetization. The logical weight of the entire edifice rests on arithmetic, from which the remainder of mathematics can be built up, as Russell and Whitehead showed in 1913. All analytic philosophy, in turn, rests on analogies with the truths of arithmetic.

But are the axioms of arithmetic consistent and complete? David Hilbert set out to prove this (that is, the absolute consistency of arithmetic, and thus mathematics) and became the father of the formalist school. The Dutchman L. E. J. Brouwer, on the other hand, championed the intuitionist school. The collision between these views led Gödel to show in the 1930s that the question addressed by Hilbert was *not answerable:* that is, proof of the absolute consistency of mathematics could never be given—it was a "fundamentally undecidable proposition." By resorting to the famous Barber Paradox of Russell, one can easily illustrate this point. Barrett the Barber put a sign in his shop window saying "Barrett the Barber is willing to shave all, and only, men unwilling to shave themselves." The paradox arises when one asks, "Who will shave Barrett?" This question is undecidable within the limited language of the sign. We therefore need a new sign to take care of Barrett ("Exclude Barrett from the above"). This change fixes the problem, essentially by putting a patch on it. But Gödel showed that, in arithmetic, the added signs can be put into another, larger arithmetic language, and that *this* language also *must* include undecidable statements. Thus, if model building in science seeks to make a formalistically exact statement, it must fail, for there is no way to prove self-consistency.

This discussion may seem like employing a philosophical howitzer to slay a literary mouse, but it is important to realize that it is *not* in the above strict sense that Lem attacks the anthropocentricity of science and the pursuit of the alien. Instead, Lem bases his thesis on the earlier positivist school of the nineteenth century. One can look upon Gödel's proof—which many consider the most important development in philosophy in this century—as a confirmation of much of the earlier work of Locke, Berkeley, and Hume. Lem's evocation of this view is sound in the sense meant by the earlier philosophers, and in the strict sense receives further support from Gödel. But it is clear that there are senses in which Lem's position does not take into account recent developments in the philosophy of science. It is certainly not true, as some seem to assume, that Lem's position in *Solaris* and in other works is the correct one and that all other treatments of aliens in science fiction must be regarded as ignorant and simplistic.

Chicken Sexing and Science Fiction

The "intuitionist" school of analytic philosophy also manifests itself in some of the science fiction works about aliens; some of the best works in the field are, in fact, intuitionist. Terry Carr's "Dance of the Changer and the Three," for example, depends on a certain intuitive sense of the alien. Some of the best passages in Asimov's flawed novel *The Gods Themselves* evoke an intuition of alienness through the sensation of floating, which, for the inhabitants of another universe, has some central meaning. (Indeed, it is worth noting that Lem himself has said that he wrote *Solaris* with "no plans, no elaborated preconceptions, no tactics, no nothing"—that is, an intuitionist sense, not an analytic one!)

My own introduction to the intuitionist school came about during my boyhood in Alabama. My relatives raised chickens, and one of the biggest events each year was the hatching of the chicks. The main problem in that industry is that of culling out the males, since they do not lay eggs. To save on corn one needs to be able to spot the males among the baby chicks immediately. But it is hard to tell the male balls of fluff from the female balls of fluff. One is therefore forced to hire a chicken sexer.

Learning to be a chicken sexer is almost entirely a nonverbal process. The master chicken sexer hands the novice a chick and says "male." The novice then feels the chick. The next chick handed the novice is a female, but in his untutored state, the novice cannot at first tell the difference. After a day or two of this, though, an odd thing happens. The novice begins to be able to tell the males from the females. He does not quite know how he does it. He picks up a sense he cannot explain or describe—a sensitivity to the aura of maleness or femaleness, I suppose. After a while he can score ninety per cent or better at separating out the males.

My introduction to the process of chicken sexing was, then, also my introduction to the intuitionist school of natural philosophy. My Aunt Mildred was a master practitioner without having ever heard of Immanuel Kant or L. E. J. Brouwer. As a method of philosophical instruction, the process was, of course, rather hard on some of the chickens, but what I absorbed has stuck with me through my scientific and literary career.

Perhaps this explains why, from my reading of philosophy, I feel that the intuitionist view has not receded in this century, but rather has come to the fore. It is certainly true that language is limiting, as are the pictures in our heads, but an obvious example of a new paradigm for casting off old pictures has emerged: quantum mechanics. It is illuminating to recall Suvin's observation on Lem: "No closed reference system, however alluring to the weary and poor in spirit, is viable in the age of relativity and post-cybernetic sciences."[2] While "post-cybernetic" may be an oblique reference to Gödel, the reference to relativity is mysterious. It was, in fact, quantum mechanics that introduced the fundamentally unknowable to modern physics. Relativity dethroned simultaneity, not certainty. And there is more to twentieth-century science than a facile open-endedness.

The lesson of modern physics is that neither a wave nor a particle picture is adequate for the description of small-scale phenomena. In a diffraction experiment, for example, electrons can appear to have wavelike properties. In other contexts their point-particle—like nature is manifest. Reality is, in other words, something beyond either category. Modern physics has now passed beyond the early wave-versus-particle riddle and used mathematics itself as a guide in evolving a sense of the quantum nature of the physical world. After a substantial period of calculation and verification, we now apply to particles terms such as "color," or "charm," and "strangeness," terms reflecting purely mathematical notions.

These intuitions are, I think, basically different from the usual "physical" intuitions physicists speak of. In practice, "physical" intuition usually means describing our models by pictures associated with particles, waves, and so on—the stuff of ordinary experience. I think Lem most effectively satirizes this habit with his library episode and the Solarists' classification of the ocean's forms as "mimoids," "symmetriads," or "extensors." It is a telling attack, but it ignores the more sophisticated facets of model building in science. Specifically, it ignores the role of mathematics, which is a more nearly universal guide than our human perceptions. It seems to me that Lem, by taking a philosophical tack from the nineteenth-century rationalists, has unnecessarily limited the argument. He has missed both Gödel and the new landscape of science in this century. By placing *Solaris* in the far future, he seems to be saying that some day we will meet an irreducible, unavoidable strangeness. (This is a prediction; because it cannot be falsified, it is not, however, a scientific statement. Solaris may always lie just around the next corner.)

I have become rather skeptical of philosophers' pronouncements on the boundaries of scientific knowledge (remember Kant's exposed *a posteriori*). This is why I prefer in fiction to take philosophical metaphors rooted in experience. In this short essay, it is difficult to convey how genuinely strange quantum mechanics is and how much it has changed the way we think about science. There is a "feel" in the evolution of our ideas of quantum mechanics. As a kind of shorthand, one might say that the world of the quantum is made up of models that fold into one another. When one simple picture fails, one goes to the next. There is a way to make the transition. But even these last two sentences fail to convey a real sense of how research is done today. The notion of enfolded models is fading, being replaced by the elaborate waltz of mathematics with data. One might even say that there is, in Lem's sense, *no* model that describes our deeper and deeper progress through the levels of nature. In this relation the paradoxical nature of quantum mechanics has become only a side issue because no one believes the pictures any longer anyhow. (Note that, even in the early days of quantum mechanics, paradox did not equal muddiness, as it does in Le Guin's "Schrödinger's Cat.")

There can be a science fiction analog to what we have learned from our experience of quantum mechanics. I would term it "learning by the expansion of categories" (or, perhaps more accurately in the case of quantum mechanics, "abandoning categories"). To the extent that order and mathematics are human categories and not alien ones, of course, this partition of the argument falls to the ground. But I suspect that quantum mechanics does represent the development of a new category of human experience. It is a new paradigm beyond anything that could plausibly have been predicted, using what in the nineteenth century would have seemed a "human" intuition.

It is likely that several science fiction works have already reflected this vision. Alas, like most writers, I am poorly read. The only example I can immediately cite is my own *In the Ocean of Night*. The conclusion of that book seeks to evoke this sense of expanding categories, and a union with the world itself, as opposed to models of it. It is important to remember that language contains only what we have learned to tell each other. Such knowledge is only a tiny subset of all we do in fact know, in the chicken-sexing sense. (And as my Aunt Mildred noted in one of her lectures to me—the notes have unfortunately been lost—what we cannot talk about is not necessarily unimportant to, or uncheckable by, others—for example, to the chickens themselves.) I remember that while writing *In the Ocean of Night* I had a sense of these implications, though I cannot say much about whether it was in the mix from the beginning. In this case I, like Lem, wrote from intuition (though not without notes and planning, paradoxically enough). I am usually unaware of the full, analytical content of my work until it is done or, indeed, long after it is done.

I have argued here that there are some weighty philosophical implications to our treatment of aliens in science fiction. There are no exclusively right answers, of course, for science fiction cannot settle such issues. My sense of *Solaris* is that it does not really talk about the physical sciences at all. There, the question of whether model building is hopelessly anthropocentric can only be settled by infinite recursion—keep trying to see whether the problem cracks, whether predictions do bear out. It is an unfortunate fact that much fiction takes the "truths" of science as absolute although they were never intended to be. Science is always provisional, yet the urge to adopt the position of *Solaris* rests, I believe, on an emotional bedrock of the sort Suvin cited, from Sartre on. I think a better understanding of *Solaris* might evolve from looking at it from the perspective of the social sciences. If in some sense the ocean were alive, then *Solaris* might, for example, be read as a reflection on the error of applying a mechanistic description to a social science, *not* to a physical one. In the social sciences, including psychology, there is a fundamental limitation: one cannot do completely reproducible experiments, even on very thin social groupings. Thus Lem's criticisms would appear to apply most directly to mechanistic social theories such as Marxism. One wonders whether the literary czars of Eastern Europe (or the Marxist critics of the West) really understand quite what Lem seems to be driving at.

My own instincts as a theoretical physicist and a writer lie with the intuitionist school. I think that anyone who participates in science comes to realize that, by expanding our categories and using the most "universal" of descriptions (and languages—that is, mathematics), we can make of ourselves something greater. We can, in other words, ingest the alien. Yet we know from Gödel that the analytic sense of knowledge will forever escape us. It seems to me that this is fertile ground for bittersweet irony. Perhaps such philosophical pursuits can lead us finally to a deeper sense of what it does mean to be logical and fragile and human.

Visionary States
and the Search for
Transcendence in Science Fiction

Robert Hunt

Recent criticism of science fiction has tended to subsume all religion under the vague category "myth."[1] Both in the criticism and in the literature itself, the wellspring of religion—the individual's religious experience—is often ignored or treated in the most cheap and obvious manner. Despite this neglect, science fiction is particularly suited to the depiction of visionary states and the religious revelations they bring or seem to bring. I shall discuss some of the reasons for this suitability and show how three writers—Ian Watson, Philip K. Dick, and Robert Silverberg—have fashioned the individual religious revelation into effective narrative material.

The novelist who elects to describe the religious experience—whether in science fiction or not—is working in a reluctant medium. How is the novel—traditionally mimetic, concerned with time, change, and visible action—to deal with the most personal, timeless, and ineffable of human experiences? If the author is not simply to deal with externals, he has to create a prose equivalent for a psychic event. The rhythms and resonances of his affective prose will attempt to make us feel something of the character's sensations. If the author succeeds, we may be swept away by his narrative, and give at least temporary emotional assent to the visions he depicts. If he fails, we may sit back, unmoved, while the train to glory leaves without us.

I shall be speaking of the "visionary state," by which I mean the state in which a character sees sights, hears sounds, feels emotions that by normal standards must be illusory, but that to him are real. This includes, but is not limited to, the state of religious or mystical ecstasy, in which the spiritual seeker is drawn toward a selfless, loving union with the Absolute, or the One, or God.[2] The mystic attains union with the divine through self-mortification and self-renunciation; whereas visionary states in general can be induced by drugs, fever, pain, and starvation—to which science fiction has added telepathy, mind control, and communion with alien intelligences. The mystic union is joyful and selfless—"religious" in the common sense of the word; but other visions may be self-centered and terrifying glimpses of the abyss beneath reality. Finally, the mystic's experience is incommunicable, an end in itself; but other visionaries may become prophets, fanatics, the founders of new religions.

The three authors I will examine all depict the visionary state; all use affective prose tempered to some degree by an ironic context. But the effects of their work are utterly dissimilar; they represent three distinct postures an author can take—which range from extreme skepticism to extreme identification—in depicting religious and metaphysical ecstasies.

Why has the 1960s vogue for visionary science fiction persisted through the materialistic 1970s? At least three characteristics of science fiction as a genre make it a fit vehicle for the depiction of religious experience:

1. Religion as subject matter is now embarrassing to most middle-class novelists and critics; it is parodied, exploited, played with, but seldom openly explored. Science fiction, however, is one of the last unembarrassed genres; authors and readers are still eager to debate the meaning of reality and the mysteries of belief, and have no fear of censure from a powerful critical establishment.

2. Science fiction has traditionally had a near-monopoly on the literary treatment of telepathy, clairvoyance, and other "psi" powers. It is almost impossible to describe such powers in action without resorting to the imagery of mystics and visionaries. A. E. van Vogt's "Asylum," Theodore Sturgeon's *More Than Human,* and Alfred Bester's *Demolished Man* (to name only classics) all have as climax scenes in which the hero's mind enters into communion with other, superior minds; in each case the language is almost indistinguishable from that of saints' raptures. Such scenes are part of science fiction's Great Tradition.

3. Science fiction inevitably redefines reality. Every work, no matter how slight, must re-create the entire universe in the image the author envisions. Implicit in the science-fictional universe is the God that created it (or the nonexistent God whose absence is made clear). From the depiction of a reordered reality to the visionary

apprehension of the forces behind that reality is a smaller step in science fiction than in the object-cluttered, mimetic universe of the traditional novel.

I shall begin with Ian Watson, the young British author whose works make frequent, always ironic use of the visionary state. Each of Watson's first three novels is constructed in this pattern: A primitive people (Amazonian Indians in *The Embedding,* Bolivian peasants in *The Martian Inca*) with a complex and intuitive relationship to nature is being threatened by the massive, bureaucratic, death-bringing technology of the United States and the Soviet Union. Alternate chapters present the primitive perception of reality (heightened by drugs, sex, and nature rituals) and the startlingly similar search for illumination by the American (or Russian or British) scientists, using computers, radio telescopes, and space probes, as well as behavior modification and other assaults on human personality. In *The Jonah Kit* the role of the "primitives" is taken by gigantic sperm whales whose methods of communication, alien to all human experience, are being probed by scientists of East and West. Each novel's structure is a complex dialectic; each chapter, elliptical and confusing in itself, illumines and is illuminated by others; each novel as a whole is informed by multiple ironies and the reverberation of symbols from one setting to another. And in each novel the goal, both of the characters and of the entire work, is transcendence—a grand pattern of superhuman reality that can be glimpsed only at particular points within the book.

The Embedding is the most complex and ambitious of these novels. The key to its unity lies in the title: "embedding" acquires ever more subtle and far-reaching connotations as the narrative progresses. In Britain a team of scientists has secretly isolated a group of children from all contact with the outside world and is teaching them an "embedded" language—one in which the sentence structure encompasses many aspects of reality simultaneously rather than sequentially—in the hope that this new language will mean a new mode of cognition. In the Amazon the Indians whose jungle home is about to be flooded by an American-built dam have an "embedded" language for the drug-induced trances of their religious rituals; but the Indians are themselves "embedded" in the jungle: its trees and birds supply their metaphors and system of logic; their world is both the object and the means of cognition. In America, meanwhile, the military-technological establishment is awaiting the arrival of a spacecraft from a distant galaxy. The aliens, when they arrive, are traders—but they want to barter not for human technology but for human languages; new languages mean new modes of perception, and by collecting languages from hundreds of worlds they hope to synthesize a language that will embody "This-Reality"—the reality in which both human and alien are "embedded"—so that they can transcend it:

> "Only at the places where the languages of different species grate together, presenting an interface of paradox, do we guess the nature of true reality and draw strength to escape. Our language moon [the repository of their findings] will finally reveal reality as a direct experience. Then we shall state the Totality. We shall stand outside of This-Reality and pursue our Bereft Love. . . ."[3]

The "Bereft Love" that obsesses the aliens is a group of beings they call the "Change Speakers," who exist tangential to ordinary reality and who disappeared from the aliens' world centuries earlier, leaving an unquenchable nostalgia and longing for reunion. As the Christian mystic seeks knowledge of and union with Christ by pushing human language to and beyond its limits of expression, so the alien traders believe that by amassing all possible systems of normal cognition they will be able to rise to a higher level of cognition and directly apprehend the transcendent. Despite the linguistic-logical terminology, their quest is as emotional, as filled with displaced eroticism, as the visions of Saint Teresa:

> "The Change Speakers are *para*-beings. We . . . feel a deep bereft "love" for them, since they phased with the twin worlds so many years ago. . . . Our signal trading quest is to cancel the great sense of their sadness, so that we . . . can be left alone again—without that vibration in our minds, imprinted so many centuries ago by their passage. . . . By this ghost of love, which is pain."[4]

And the speaker, telling of their loss, stands "bound up in an alien agony, Cross and Crucified united in the same tall dry form."[5]

The aliens are not the only searchers for salvation. The Amazonian Indians await the birth of a messiah, a personification of their hallucinogenic drug who will be born with complete mastery of their "embedded" language, who will be able to manipulate reality and save them from the destruction of their home. The entire tribe is drugging itself to a different level of perception, and a French anthropologist from whose point of view they are presented muses on the effects of the hallucinogen in terms nearly identical to those used by the alien spokesman:

> He must have emerged from the experience at some particular time, he reasoned. Yet the boundary wasn't definable. The greater could not be bounded by the lesser. The perception of last night could not be imprisoned in terms of today's perception, when it was a vaster, more devastating mode of perception. Thus its bounds could not be set. How could a two-dimensional being who had been able to experience three dimensions set up a frontier post anywhere in his flat territory—and say beyond this point lies the Other? For the Other would be everywhere—and nowhere, to him.[6]

Like the aliens, the Indians desire to move at right angles to reality—and so, in his own quest, does the British psychologist, the ironically named Christopher Sole, the first of the series of world-weary, sexually discontented researchers who carry the banner of modern science in Watson's novels. His children are "programmed" to manufacture new systems of cognition, to "test the frontiers of reality." Yet, even as he manipulates them, Sole loves them, sees them as a new messianic breed able to save mankind from the futility of information-glutted modern life. His affection, like all emotions in *The Embedding*—the Frenchman's affection for the Indians, the Indians' faith in their messiah, the aliens' hope for transcendence—is misplaced and ultimately self-destructive.

From the first page of *The Embedding* the novel's three plots begin to coalesce and interact; finally they explode—figuratively and literally—against one another. One dream after another is betrayed and aborted. The characters are too deeply embedded in circumstance ever to transcend it. They are not the godlike aliens of so much science fiction, nor the noble savages of romantic anthropology; all are fragments, different aspects of dissatisfied, searching, self-defeating modern man.

The world view of *The Embedding* is echoed in *The Jonah Kit*, in which an astronomer proposes that our universe is an afterthought, an accidental creation that God has forgotten. Nor is there any lasting transcendence in *The Martian Inca*, in which peasants in the Bolivian desert and astronauts in the Martian desert both experience a spiritual illumination and rebirth—and rush blindly after their self-destructive messianic dreams.

"This-Reality," Watson's novels suggest, is inescapable. The attempt to define it is solipsism; the attempt to transcend it creates a pattern of action that—like the physical universe—curves back upon itself. The search for "*para*-reality," abandoned since the death of religion as a force in the Western world, may be mankind's next crusade and final delusion. Our "embedding" in the muck and venality of the world we know is part of what defines us.

For all their mind-numbing metaphysical legerdemain, Watson's novels are at bottom materialistic; his subject is not revelation so much as the impossibility of revelation. By contrast, in the works of Philip K. Dick, revelation is a part of the landscape—it is something that happens to his characters whether they are actively seeking it or (as is usually the case) are simply trying to stay alive and make a living.

More than any other science fiction writer, Dick has a sense of the reality of good and evil. They are qualities that take human form and that affect human lives. Evil in particular is tangible ("like cement," says Mr. Tagomi in *The Man in the High Castle*); it is the principle of destruction, loss of coherence, entropy. Against the background of pervasive evil the quality of good is fragile and elusive; there is some in Dick's desperately bumbling heroes, more in the women they love, but most in the artists and artisans—potters, musicians, tinkerers, small-time craftsmen—who are the only forces of creation and continuity in Dick's universe.

With the introduction of drugs, telepathy, precognition, or nuclear disaster, observable reality changes, revealing new realities that may themselves be illusions. People and objects undergo metamorphosis or rapid decay, time runs backward, the course of events unravels and rearranges itself. Amid this flux of realities the transcendent forces at work in the world flash into momentary visibility.

The dominant theme in a number of Dick's works is the vision of an evil and destructive—and perhaps omnipotent—God, the worst Manichean nightmare come true. This malignant, all-seeing deity is the eponymous vision of *Eye in the Sky* (1957), but in that novel it is clearly the product of one character's psychosis. By the time of *The Three Stigmata of Palmer Eldritch* (1965), Dick has deliberately blurred the distinction between madness and revelation. In *The Three Stigmata* a dying Earth keeps its Martian colonists dependent by supplying them with Can-D, a hallucinogenic drug that enables them to live the fantasy lives of twentieth-century consumers. The drug monopoly is shattered by the return from Proxima Centauri of industrialist Palmer Eldritch with a competing drug: Chew-Z. But Chew-Z offers, not an escape into fantasy, but a descent into the depths of metaphysical reality. When Leo Bulero, the Can-D tycoon, tries to confront Eldritch, he is abducted and injected with Chew-Z; he finds himself temporarily in a world that Eldritch has imagined and in which Eldritch has almost godlike powers. Bulero also has a vision of the future, and believes that *he* will be the man who killed Palmer Eldritch and saved the solar system from the new drug's effects. This hope, offered early in the novel, fades before a new revelation: the form of Palmer Eldritch is inhabited by an alien intelligence that is inexorably seeping into reality.

Long before Eldritch appears in the flesh, his three stigmata haunt the novel: his slotted camera eyes, steel teeth, and mechanical right arm. Bulero perceives these stigmata as "the evil, negative trinity of alienation, blurred reality, and despair."[7] But Eldritch is no simple figure of evil; his name combines *palmer,* a pilgrim who has returned from the Holy Land, with *eldritch,* weird or uncanny; as the hero, Barney Mayerson, suggests, Eldritch contains both the divine and the terrible. Whether through malice or weakness, Eldritch's image increasingly penetrates reality; people decay into Palmer Eldritch, acquiring the dead eyes, mechanical jaw, and crushing steel grip that set him apart.

In the figure of Eldritch we must deal with the author's most personal and deeply felt symbolism. In a speech written for a science fiction conference in 1975, Dick described a religious vision:

> Think of the war-mask which Pericles placed over his features: you would behold a frozen visage, the grimness of war, without compassion—no genuine human face or person to whom you could appeal. . . . Now, this is almost exactly how I described Palmer Eldritch in my novel about him: so much like the war-mask of the Attic Greeks that the resemblance cannot be accidental. Is, then, the hollow eyeslot, the mechanical metal arm and hand, the stainless steel teeth, which are the dread stigmata of evil—is this not, this which I myself first saw in the overhead sky at noon one day back in 1963, a description, a vision, of a war-mask and metal armour, a god of battle? The God of Wrath who was angry with me.[8]

Looking at *The Three Stigmata* with a decade's perspective, Dick suggested that the terrible mask might conceal the face of "a kind and loving man." But in the novel itself Eldritch incarnates the God of entropy, destructive and ultimately beyond human understanding. "I'd like to know," asks Barney Mayerson, "what you were trying to do when you introduced Chew-Z to our people." "Perpetuate myself," answers the entity in Eldritch's form. "Don't fret about that now, Mr. Mayerson. . . . Just tend your little garden."⁹ And with this Voltairean rebuke to human curiosity it leaves Barney feeling "unclean," contaminated by Eldritch, wondering whether any sacrament can mediate between man and God, whether God can ever be convinced of His responsibility.

Dick presents an even more disturbing vision in the story "Faith of Our Fathers" (1967). In the all-Communist world of the narrative, "faith" means unquestioning devotion to the idolized Mao-like leader. Chien, a minor party official, wants to penetrate the veil of lies and contradictions that surrounds the leader; he takes, not a hallucinogen, but an antihallucinogen, hoping to break free from the drug-induced euphoria in which the party faithful are kept. Others have perceived the leader as an alien or a machine; what Chien sees is far more frightening:

> It was terrible; it blasted him with its awfulness. As it moved it drained the life from each person in turn; it ate the people who had assembled, passed on, ate again, ate more with an endless appetite. It hated; he felt its hate. It loathed; he felt its loathing for everyone present—in fact he shared its loathing. . . . I know who you are, Tung Chien thought to himself. You, the supreme head of the world-wide Party structure. You, who destroy whatever living object you touch. . . . You go anywhere, appear anytime, devour anything; you engineer life and then guzzle it, and you enjoy that.
> He thought, You are God.¹⁰

Chien had hoped to verify the visions of others; instead, he experiences a revelation that renders all life and effort futile. As in *The Three Stigmata of Palmer Eldritch,* perception *is* reality: Chien's vision places a pseudohand on his shoulder and leaves bleeding wounds—the stigmata of the man who has seen too much. The story ends with Chien in bed with the one woman he can trust, desperately making love, affirming his own sense of reality while the terror underlying the universe slowly bleeds him to death.

What are we to make of the revelations with which Dick's heroes are afflicted? Dick reverses the Berkeleian dictum (and starting point of the traditional novel) *esse est percipi;* in his fictional universe, *to be perceived* is to be: every perceived reality is, at some time and to some degree, true. Thus God as Goodness and the God of Wrath are alternate aspects of the human experience; each is alternately the truth with which we live.

The paradox of the dual God is shown explicitly in Dick's recent collaboration with Roger Zelazny, *Deus Irae.* The failure of the collaboration to jell leaves Dick's part of the narrative unusually clear. In a postbomb America (clearly inspired by Walter Miller's *Canticle for Leibowitz*) a crippled mutant goes in search of Carlton Lufteufel, The Man Who Dropped The Bomb. Lufteufel, as his name indicates, is the devil, the principle of destruction made flesh, but he is also worshipped as *Deus Irae,* the God of Wrath; the mutant's task is to meet this deity face to face and to paint the terrible visage. The novel's severest fault is that Lufteufel's mode of existence is never clear: is he a madman worshipped by fanatics, or in some sense supernatural? The ambiguity seems careless rather than deliberate; in Zelazny's scenes Lufteufel is thoroughly mortal, but elsewhere his metallic visage appears in the sky, an apparition closely modeled on Dick's own vision of the God of Wrath. And after Lufteufel's death it is indeed as though the God of Wrath, and with him the principles of original sin and retribution, has disappeared from human experience; a pall lifts from the Earth and from the hearts of men and women.

The novel's oddly moving coda reflects Dick's more recent view of the immanence of Good. The spiritual spring at the end of *Deus Irae* is one example of the voice that cries "Sleepers, awake!" to the creative impulse within plants, animals, and humans.[11] The tentative optimism of this pantheistic world view was implicit in many of Dick's earlier novels (for example, *The Man in the High Castle* and *Now Wait for Last Year*), but was overshadowed by powerful images of evil. *A Scanner Darkly,* his most recent novel, suggests that Dick's future work, while ambiguous and visionary as ever, will take a more hopeful view of the uneasy relationship between God and man.

Watson uses visionary states to express a profound skepticism; Dick is wry and ambiguous; but Robert Silverberg in two novels presents powerful visions that seem to demand that we accept them as valid. To be sure, Silverberg also deals ironically with religious themes: the android messiah in *Tower of Glass,* the messiah from the future in *The Masks of Time,* the cult of immortality in *The Book of Skulls*—all destroy the believers that flock to them; similarly, the psychedelic ecstasies of *The World Inside* are technologically induced, a sterile, nontranscendent opiate of the masses. All these novels, however, share Silverberg's theme of messianism: their heroes—intellectual, alienated, hypersexual—are driven to search for something greater and more real than themselves. In *Downward to the Earth* and *A Time of Changes,* the heroes find the transcendence they seek. In both these novels the transcendence is achieved through drugs—not the treacherous Alice-in-Wonderland pills of Dick's novels, but organic brews (as in Watson's *Embedding* and *Martian Inca*) with the power to transform the human soul. The visible sign of the heroes' new life is their intimate communion with others: in *A Time of Changes* communion between humans; in *Downward to the Earth,* between human and alien.

A Time of Changes is set on a harshly hostile planet inhabited by descendants of Earthmen. The discipline needed for survival has caused them to banish all forms of self-expression from language and life: the pronouns *I* and *me* are obscenities; to speak of one's own feelings, ambitions, or desires is to be guilty of "selfbaring," a crime punished by ostracism or death. The hero-narrator has learned to break down this barrier to individuality by means of a forbidden drug that induces a temporary telepathic state. The novel itself is his testament, written in the first person and embodying in its very narrative voice the new dimension of self-expression.

Kinnall Darival is a feudal prince, self-exiled and bitter, whose alienation from others is expressed in his awkwardness and sexual inadequacy. He is introduced to the "selfbaring" drug by an Earthman named Schweiz and experiences for the first time the topography of another's soul:

> I passed through the strata of Schweiz's soul, inspecting the gritty layers of greed and the boulders of trickery, the oily pockets of maliciousness, the decaying loam of opportunism. Here was self incarnate; here was a man who had lived solely for his own sake.
>
> Yet I did not recoil from the darkness of Schweiz.
>
> I saw beyond those things. I saw the yearning, the god-hunger in the man. . . . Sly and opportunistic he might be, yes, but also vulnerable, passionate, honest beneath all his capering. I could not judge Schweiz harshly. He was I. I was

> he. Tides of self engulfed us both. If I were to cast Schweiz
> down, I must also cast down Kinnall Darival. My soul was
> flooded with warmth for him.[12]

Kinnall's second experience of the drug is with a prostitute. This
communion is simultaneously sexual and spiritual: Kinnall feels
himself both male and female, experiences her orgasm together with
his own. In this novel's world of discourse there is nothing illusory
about these ecstasies. Kinnall enters totally into the minds and souls
of others and finds that to commune with another is inevitably to
love that person. He dreams of becoming a messiah, a missionary of
soul-baring, giving the drug to all and making thousands of converts,
utterly transforming the society that produced him.

Kinnall's last communion is with his "bondsister," a married
woman for whom he has long felt a forbidden love. Again, the
metaphors are topographical:

> I found myself . . . in corridors with glassy floors and silvered
> walls, through which there played a cool sparkling light, like
> the crystalline brightness one sees reflected from the white
> sandy bottom of a shallow tropical cove. This was Halum's
> virginal inwardness. In niches along these corridors, neatly
> displayed, were the shaping factors of her life, memories,
> images, odors, tastes, visions, fantasies, disappointments, de-
> lights. A prevailing purity governed everything.[13]

But this communion overwhelms Halum and drives her to suicide;
Kinnall flees to the desert, where like a biblical prophet he examines
his soul and writes his testament while awaiting capture. Kinnall's
final vision is of his book surviving him, spreading his doctrine,
making converts in spite of persecution:

> I saw the bright glow encompassing the world, shimmering,
> flickering, gaining power, deepening in hue. I saw walls
> crumbling. I saw the brilliant red blaze of universal love. I
> saw new faces, changed and exultant. Hands touching hands.
> Selves touching selves. . . . It has happened before. I will
> disappear, I the forerunner, I the anticipator, I the martyred
> prophet. But what I have written will live, and through me
> you will be changed. It may yet be that this is no idle dream.[14]

"Go and love," Kinnall bids his imagined readers. "Go and be open. Go and be healed.'' From the narrative's triumphant conclusion we are forced to assume that this new faith will supplant the repressive Covenant as surely as Christianity spread throughout the Roman Empire. But, although Kinnall is its Christ, this is a Christianity without dogma, commandments, or sanctions; most significantly, it is a religion without a real God. For although Kinnall Darival experiences the classic mystic union—ecstatic, loving, selfless—this union is with other men and women, not with any supernatural entity. God is in humanity: we are God—that is the inevitable (and inevitably disappointing) inference we draw from *A Time of Changes;* and although the novel has its ironies (the skillfully depicted confusion between selflessness and self-absorption is one of them), no irony undermines the anthropocentric optimism of its conclusion.

A close parallel to Kinnall's spiritual pilgrimage is the quest of Gundersen, an Earthman returning for atonement to a planet he has helped despoil, in *Downward to the Earth.* The planet has two dominant species: the elephantlike ''nildor''—massive, patient, and benignly wise—and the savage, apelike ''sulidor.'' This dichotomy of species carries echoes of Swift's Houyhnhms and Yahoos or Wells's Eloi and Morlocks. Like Gulliver among the Houyhnhms, Gundersen wants to abase himself before the nildor, to participate in their ritual of ''rebirth'' in hope that it will destroy him as it has destroyed other Earthmen. Instead, the ritual drug produces a revelation: sulidor and nildor are one species, periodically metamorphosing from the carnal to the spiritual form and back again. At the novel's climax Gundersen has an ecstatic vision of the unity of all thinking creatures and of the continuity of life:

> He hears the tolling of mighty bells.
> He feels the planet shuddering and shifting on its axis.
> He smells dancing tongues of flame.
> He touches the roots of the rebirth mountain.
> He feels the souls of nildoror and sulidoror all
>   about him.
> He recognizes the words of the hymn the sulidoror sing,
>   and he sings with them.
> He grows. He shrinks. He burns. He shivers. He changes.[15]

Gundersen, too, undergoes a metamorphosis, but in his new mode of perception the physical and spiritual are metaphors for each other:

> Gundersen [looking in a mirror] stared at the mask-like face
> with hooded slots for eyes, at the slitted nose, the gill-
> pouches trailing to his shoulders, the many-jointed arms, the
> row of sensors on the chest, the grasping organs at the hips,
> the cratered skin, the glow organs in the cheeks. He looked
> down at himself and saw none of those things. . . . He saw
> himself, and it was his old body he saw, and then he flickered
> and underwent a phase shift and he beheld the being with
> sensors and slots, and then he was himself again.[16]

His amphibious form and extra senses symbolize Gundersen's new
ability to move in both the physical and the spiritual worlds. As the
novel ends he descends the mountain, ready to preach his discovery
to a waiting universe. The scene has mythic echoes (Moses descend-
ing Horeb and Sinai, Zarathustra coming down from the mountain to
preach the *Übermensch*) and Gundersen is self-consciously a new
Christ:

> A vision of a mankind transformed blazed within him. I am
> the emissary, he thought. I am the bridge over which they
> shall cross. I am the resurrection and the life. I am the light of
> the world: he that followeth me shall not walk in darkness,
> but shall have the light of life. A new commandment I give
> unto you, that ye love one another.[17]

The novel's title is from Ecclesiastes: "Who knoweth the spirit of
man that goeth upward, and the spirit of the beast that goeth downward to the earth?" As in *A Time of Changes,* the new doctrine is
that of unity: the spirit of man and beast (so violently separated in
Gulliver's Travels or *The Time Machine*) will be united under the
new dispensation, the new religion of which Gundersen is the messiah. But (again as in *A Time of Changes*) there is religious feeling
without a true religion. Heaven, revelation, transfiguration are all to
occur in *this* life; paradise and perfection seem to be implicit in all
intelligent beings.

Silverberg keeps the triumphant affirmations of these two novels
scrupulously free of irony. If we as readers cannot accept the
heroes' spiritual transformations as plausible and proper, we must
reject the novels, for there is no alternative explanation or viewpoint
for us to fall back on. Indeed, there is no one to express such a
viewpoint; Silverberg's messianic novels are constructed so rigorously from the hero's perspective that the other characters are

shadows by comparison. The questing male ego that dominates Silverberg's works finds its fulfillment in *A Time of Changes* and *Downward to the Earth;* for the reader, however, the fulfillment is self-referential: the novels are complete and satisfying in their own terms, but those terms bear only the vaguest relation to the world outside the narrative. In the manner (although not in the spirit) of Lem's critiques of unwritten books, Silverberg has written bibles for unfounded religions.

I began by defining the problem of portraying visionary states in the novel: how can an objective, mimetic genre deal with a private, subjective, incommunicable experience? Watson, Dick, and Silverberg have provided part of the answer: with ironic structure and artful ambiguity, with sophisticated affective prose, with sensitivity to the mythic resonances of religious experience, the visionary state and those who undergo it can be shaped into effective narrative material. That this material sometimes leaves us intellectually unsatisfied or unsure of our own critical response reflects, not the limitations of the subject matter, but the success or failure of individual works of fiction and of visionary values in our own eyes.

These authors have also shown that the conventions of science fiction are essential to their art. Alien intelligences, telepathy, and reality-altering drugs are not empty clichés or concessions to an immature audience; they are as vital to the works I have discussed as such "conventions" as railroads, the middle class, or the Church of England were to the novelists of the nineteenth century. The objective obsessions of our age have tended to banish serious religious speculation from prose fiction—both from the "literary" novel and the grocery-store novel. Science fiction, which from the beginning has transcended the mimetic strictures of the genre, is at present the true literary home of visionary states and religious experience, and gives every sign of remaining so.

Fairy Tales and Science Fiction

Eric S. Rabkin

"The Frog Prince" begins, "In the old times, when it was still of some use to wish for the thing one wanted. . . ."[1] Wish fulfillment, the omnipotence of thought, and the illusion of central position are concepts that we have had named for us by Freud and Piaget but that functioned time out of mind in the fairy tales of children. As infants wanting food, we were fed; wanting warmth, we were covered; wanting comfort, we were held. Small wonder then that the time of wish fulfillment is the past before memory. But the time of the imagined-made-real could just as easily be the future beyond memory. Nathaniel Hawthorne begins "Earth's Holocaust" (1844), "Once upon a time—but whether in the time past or time to come is a matter of little or no moment." Hawthorne's pessimistic allegory describes an archetypal bonfire in which humanity tries to destroy all the artifacts that make up our corrupt civilization—but not everything can be purged: "Death . . . is an idea that cannot easily be dispensed with in any condition between the primal innocence and that other purity and perfection which perchance we are destined to attain after traveling round the full circle."[2] If we inhabit a world that manifestly urges escape, it is clear that our satisfactions lie either behind or before us:

> "The rule is, jam tomorrow and jam yesterday—but never jam *to-day*."
>
> "It *must* come sometimes to 'jam to-day,' " Alice objected.
>
> "No, it can't," said the Queen. "It's jam every *other* day: to-day isn't any *other* day, you know."[3]

If our world is not as we would like it, if we want to inhabit some other day, it is equally the job of the fairy tales of our past and the science fictions of our future to provide us with sweet preserves.

In his excellent book on fairy tales called *Once Upon a Time* (1970), Max Lüthi points out that miracles, which are both astonishing and central to legends, are a matter of course in fairy tales. This agrees completely with J. R. R. Tolkien's famous notion of the spell-bound world of Faërie described in his essay called "On Fairy Stories" (in *Tree and Leaf*, 1964). Miracles are just as easily accepted in science fiction as they are in fairy tales, as anyone knows who has read of the intervention of deity in the affairs of humanity in Olaf Stapledon's *Star Maker* (1937), Arthur C. Clarke's *Childhood's End* (1953), or James Blish's *A Case of Conscience* (1958). More generally, the minor miracles of faster-than-light travel, reanimation of the dead, and telepathy occur in science fictionland with the same regularity that wished-for places appear, dead mothers return as godmothers, and animals respond to human desire in fairyland. Hawthorne recognized the persistent power of fairy tales to function after much had apparently been done to them. His narrator watching the bonfire is "amazed"

> to observe how indefinite was the proportion between the physical mass of any given author and the property of brilliant and long-continued combustion. . . . not a quarto volume of the last century . . . could compete in that particular with a child's little gilt-covered book, containing Mother Goose's Melodies. The Life and Death of Tom Thumb outlasted the biography of Marlborough.[4]

We can all agree to the permanence of the appeal of fairy tales. Hawthorne's bonfire does not finally purge evil because it has not touched "the human heart," but when Ray Bradbury reuses that bonfire in "The Million-Year Picnic," last of the stories comprising *The Martian Chronicles* (1946; 1950), the father is successful in "burning a way of life" and turning himself and his family into "Martians," purified humans only slightly distinguishable from the rejuvenated innocent whom R. W. B. Lewis called "the American Adam" in his book by that title (1955). The miracle is a matter of course in science fiction, just as it has always been in fairy tales.

Although both fairy tales and science fictions have been studied often, the significance of the one for the other has gone almost undiscussed. Those interested in fairy tales, such as Bruno Bettelheim (*The Uses of Enchantment,* 1976) Max Lüthi, and Roger Sale (*Fairy Tales and After,* 1978), leave science fiction unexplored; those interested in science fiction, such as Brian Aldiss (*Billion Year Spree,* 1973), James Gunn (*Alternate Worlds,* 1975), and I (*Science Fiction: History, Science, Vision,* with Robert Scholes, 1977) rarely mention fairy tales as significant background. But the coincidence of wish fulfillment and temporal domains in both science fictions and fairy tales is no accident. As Arthur C. Clarke has often mentioned, a "sufficiently advanced technology is indistinguishable from magic."[5] The literature of sufficiently advanced technology is called science fiction. The ample correspondence between science fiction and fairy tales has led to frequent similarities in stylistic technique, audience attitude, character of the protagonist, choice of motif, and overall structure. We can consider these matters one by one.

Two of the most persistent stylistic traits of fairy tales are the propensity to externalize all inner states and to deal in extremes. Beauty is not just skin deep but represents superior worth. Cinderella is not merely good but also beautiful; her stepsisters are ugly in spirit as well as in body. Snow White is not the second prettiest seven-year-old in East Paramus, New Jersey, but quite decidedly "the fairest of us all." When adult values appear to conflict with this external logic, beauty always wins. For example, in the Grimms' tale "The Three Spinsters," a mother lies in declaring her daughter's extreme industriousness to the Queen. The Queen sets an impossible spinning task as a prerequisite to marriage to the Prince. The lazy girl by chance is aided by three ugly, old, unmarried women on the condition that they be invited to the wedding. At the ensuing wedding the Prince asks about them, and the girl explains that their deformities are the result of years of toil at spindle and wheel, so "then the bridgegroom said that from that time forward his beautiful bride should never touch a spinning-wheel. And so she escaped that tiresome flax-spinning."[6] In the world of fairy tales, it is clearly better to be beautiful than truthful.

Some fairy tales seem at first glance to offer a more sophisticated view. In "The Frog Prince" the Princess is required by her father the King to accept the ugly creature, and in "The Ram," Countess D'Aulnoy's highly literary version of "Beauty and the Beast" (1698), Beast wins over Beauty by his kindness. But notice that, although the Princess is ordered to accept the frog, in fact "she threw him with all her strength against the wall. . . . But as he fell, he ceased to be a frog, and became all at once a prince with beautiful kind eyes. And it came to pass that, with her father's consent, they became bride and bridegroom.''[7] In "The Ram" Beauty's kiss and declaration of love come too late; Beast is untransformed and Beauty dies of grief. Neither of these stories, though apparently asking us to look beneath the skin, returns happiness for the recognition of inner beauty.

So-called mainstream fiction often recognizes the inner worth of unlovely characters. The unmanned Uncle Toby of Laurence Sterne's *Tristram Shandy* (1760–67), the epileptic Prince Myshkin of Feodor Dostoevsky's *The Idiot* (1866), and the large-eared and "elongated" Yakov Bok of Bernard Malamud's *The Fixer* (1966)— just to name three who span the centuries and the nations—each provide a moral center for the novels they inhabit. Science fiction, on the other hand, even when flirting with such antimaterialistic notions, typically reveals its fairy tale origins. By one argument, for example, the demon provides the moral center in Mary Shelley's *Frankenstein* (1818). He is clearly superior to his *Doppelgänger* and creator, Victor. The unnamed creation is a Rousseauean Noble Savage and exhibits all the innate knowledge of the Natural Man: "I had admired the perfect forms of my cottagers—their grace, beauty, and delicate complexions: but how was I terrified when I viewed myself in a transparent pool! . . . when I became fully convinced that I was in reality the monster that I am."[8] Here again the recognition of inner worth leads not at all to happiness. Yakov Bok's endurance is made to seem the moral stimulus for the Russian Revolution, but the demon's kindness is so out of consort with his ugliness that he is driven to murder. Thus his ugliness not only prevents him from attaining the happy marriage accorded the beautiful characters in fairy tales, but it also leads him to the acquirement of enough guilt to fundamentally mitigate his moral position. In the last analysis, community itself provides the moral center in Shelley's novel: Robert Walton is superior to Victor Frankenstein because, where the latter spurns the advice of his friends and family and causes tragedy, the former finally acquiesces to the demands of his crew and safely turns back from his doomed voyage of Arctic discovery. When Isaac Asimov wants to break down his readers' fear of the nonhuman, he displays in *I, Robot* (1950) a character named Stephen Byerley who may or may not be a robot . In any event, he is surely good and, as shown in the story "Evidence" (1946), physically appealing: "The face of Stephen Byerley is not an easy one to describe. He was forty by birth certificate and forty by appearance— but it was a healthy, well-nourished good-natured appearance of forty. . . . This was particularly true when he laughed, and he was laughing now.''[9] At its pulpiest, science fiction frequently reveals its fairy tale origins by reducing beauty and ugliness to humans and Bug-Eyed-Monsters.

Another persistent stylistic trait of fairy tales is the reliance on clarity, elemental colors, and cleanliness. No matter how many villains get rolled downhill in barrels studded inside with nails, no blood flows from between the slats. When blood is mentioned, as when Snow White's mother pricks her finger, exactly three drops fall, each purely red—and they never dry brown. Lüthi asserts, ''The fairy tale portrays an imperishable world, and this explains its partiality for everything metallic and mineral, for gold and crystal.''[10] This is how Ray Bradbury describes the life of a Martian couple before the profane advent of Earthmen:

> They had a house of crystal pillars on the planet Mars by the edge of an empty sea, and every morning you could see Mrs. K eating the golden fruits that grew from the crystal walls . . . and the wine trees stood stiff in the yard, and . . . Mr. K himself in his room, reading from a metal book with raised hieroglyphs over which he brushed his hand, as one might play a harp. And from the book, as his fingers stroked, a voice sang, a soft ancient voice, which told tales of when the sea was red steam on the shore and ancient men had carried clouds of metal insects and electric spiders into battle.[11]

Not every work of science fiction, of course, conjures up so rich a broth of medievalism, singing harps and sacred texts, but surely we do recognize science fiction in general as the domain of blazing stars, coal-black space, red Mars, green Venus, and blue Earth.

Lüthi writes, ''The fairy tale portrays a clearly and neatly fashioned world . . . . The very fact that it prefers castle and city to village and cave shows its predilection for what has been formed and created by the mind of man.''[12] The mind of man has created many things, of course, including radios, ray guns, and space ships: for our discussion, space ships above all. Lüthi himself notes that technology, and particularly the technology of transport, makes our modern world very like a fairy tale.[13] James Gunn, in discussing how technology has changed the world all writers must write about, observes that the future once predicted by science fiction is ''so significantly like our present that we can say we are today living in a science fiction world.''[14] Whether technology has made ours into a world of fairyland or of science fictionland seems in part a matter of point of view. Stephen Spielberg delivers the Gospel from Outer Space in his film *Close Encounters* (1977), and C. G. Jung explains how we have developed a mundane psychic need for such a message in his book *Flying Saucers* (1959). Call the beasts that haunt our land dragons and wizards or call them mutations and mad scientists, the elemental need for fiction to deal with the beasts we feel in our world does not go away; fictions tailored to fulfill that need, quite properly, share many traits of style.

Fairy tales and science fiction serve audiences that share certain characteristics. Fairy tales clearly indulge our fascination with the magical. Science fiction has had precisely the opposite claim made for it. The first great science fiction editor, Hugo Gernsback, wrote often of his magazines as vehicles for prophecy; F. Orlin Tremaine, another early editor, wrote that "we must so plan that twenty years hence it will be said that *Astounding Stories* has served as the cradle of modern science."[15] Although these editors served their readers stories full of scientific-sounding explanations, the real motive for reading the stories was not to learn science but to experience the "astounding" (or, for that matter, to cite other magazine titles, the "amazing," the "fantastic," the "astonishing," and the "weird"). In short, science fictions, just like fairy tales, serve our interests in the magical.

"Hansel and Grethel," despite the fact that the title characters partially eat a house, risk being eaten, and finally cook a witch, is not fundamentally about food. The children are abandoned in the forest under the instigation of their stepmother, and when they return after roasting the witch the stepmother is found to have died. The logic of this is scientifically flawed but subjectively valid: "Hansel and Grethel" is about the guilt associated with children's possessiveness about their parents, especially a girl's desires for her father. By splitting the figure of the mature woman into two characters, Grethel—and through her a girl-listener—is able to have the fiction deal effectively with this guilt. In Robert A. Heinlein's *The Puppet Masters,* we have in part a Cold War allegory. The scientific fact of the alien slugs' ability to control human minds is no more valid than the coincidental death of the stepmother. Equally unreasonable is the assertion that the protagonist, Sam Nevins, can survive being "slug-ridden" while almost no one else can. But these scientific cavils are not to the point. Subjectively Heinlein has used the figure of the slugs to split off the unreasonably restraining aspects of one's father from the nurturing aspects of the parent dramatized in Sam's

government boss, known as "the Old Man." His boss is later re-
vealed to be his actual father and, matured by fighting the slugs on
Earth, Sam is empowered to lead the expedition to their "nest" on
Saturn's satellite of Titan. The book ends with these words:

> We are about to transship. I feel exhilarated. Puppet
> masters—the free men are coming to kill you!
> *Death and Destruction!*[16]

In a simple sense these free men are good, anti-Communist Americans; but in the deeper and more important subjective sense, they
have been freed to lash out at that aspect of their parents that had
previously unjustly restrained them. As in the fairy tale, the scientific logic is not to the point: the fiction, by the technique of distribut-
ing the qualities of one role into two figures, makes possible the
creation of a subjective security. Fairy tale audiences and science
fiction audiences often share the need for this subjective drama.

Fairy tales and science fictions are often highly formulaic. The
security of literary form is most potent in formula literature—so long
as a reader is not too sophisticated to enjoy the formula or can
suspend his sophistication for the art's sake. Hence the formal
power of these genres should be equally present in other genres that
use or derive from well-established formulae. Westerns stories and
detective fictions come to mind. Detective fictions, of course, often
have even more the veneer of scientific explanation than do science
fictions. And yet, can any of us soberly assent outside the fictions to
such assertions as Poirot's that "there isn't such a thing as a mur-
derer who commits crimes at random"?[17] As for Westerns, we need
not even look beyond science fiction itself: John Carter, Edgar Rice
Burroughs' cowboy on Mars, is only one in a long line of resourceful
loners who offer the identifying reader not so much scientific
prophecy as a chance to feel important. In Space Opera and in
Sword-and-Sorcery, at least, science fiction functions in precisely
the way Bettelheim suggests that fairy tales do, providing not so
much logical answers as satisfying ones.[18] The popularity of George
Lucas' *Star Wars* (1977) is not based solely on special effects.

Paul A. Carter gathered together much of the survey information
available concerning the readership of science fiction. In 1940 editor
Jerry Westerfield wrote that "the science fiction reader is usually a
boy in his late teens," and another editor suggested that "90% of our
readers are masculine youngsters who are learning and who don't
know just what to believe and what not to believe." In short, they do

not so much want explanations that open up new problems as they want fictions that handle their old problems. While surely this assessment does not cover all science fiction or all science fiction readers or even the totality of the experience of any given reading, science fiction writer Joanna Russ could assert as late as 1970 that most readers of science fiction are "young" and "male."[19] This particular type of reader seems to respond frequently to a protagonist who shares with the typical fairy tale protagonist the receipt—often undeserved—of magical gifts or help and participates in a plot that makes his own position clearly central to the world he inhabits.

The Gallant Tailor, who vaingloriously announces that he killed "seven at one blow!" is an inconsiderate, nasty, and finally unrestrained individual, but he is, in the words of the story, "nimble," or, as we would say, "shrewd"; and so, after defeating his moral and physical superiors by trickery, "the little tailor all his lifetime remained a king." The whole kingdom—read "world"—depends on him. Fairy tales almost universally indulge the so-called illusion of central position, and often so do science fictions. Lloyd Biggle's lone Earthman on a Tahiti-like planet in *Monument* (1974) is typical: "he was the one man in the cosmos who knew how to save this world and this people, and he could not do it because he was dying. . . . he had to make decisions that would affect the entire future of his people and his world, and the thought of a wrong choice terrified him."[20] At the surface level, the novel concerns the Plan that the Earthman leaves for the natives to follow in thwarting the spoliation of their world by others, but below the surface Biggle has given us a story that asks whether or not, in a world of powerful political forces, it is still possible for a single man—the reader perhaps—to lay plans that will work. We all feel sometimes that we do not have enough strength, that we might well be wrong; *Monument* tells us it is worth the try. Like fairy tales, science fictions accord us, through the protagonists, the central position.

Like the protagonists of fairy tales, the protagonists of science fictions may not be at all deserving of their central position. Biggle's hero wins our respect because he cares so much, but the great forces of the universe conduct Stapledon's "disembodied viewpoint" on his cosmic tour (*Star Maker,* 1937) not because he deserves enlightenment but because they want to enlighten. Spider Robinson has created in *Callahan's Crosstime Saloon* (1977), a place in which a troubled person can tell his tale, and, by virtue of being the center of everyone's attention, be miraculously helped. This is clearly a fairy tale arrangement: "It's almost as though some sort of protective spell ensures that the only people who find Callahan's are the ones who should—and the ones who must."[21] The central position is accorded even to so undeserving a character as one who comes into Callahan's initially to rob it.

Often the central position of the narrator correlates with a trait parallel to the Gallant Tailor's shrewdness. Science fiction is chockablock with boy scientists who invent their way out of trouble. Hugo Gernsback's Ralph 124C41+ is "one of the greatest living scientists and *one of the ten men on the whole planet earth permitted to use the Plus sign after his name*" (Gernsback's italics).[22] Although this may not make Ralph, in true fairy tale fashion, the absolutely smartest person in the universe, by the end of the novel he has matured and in the last chapter "remained conscious by sheer force of will."[23] Ralph's brains, however, are his not by virtue but by chance—a fact most readers overlook. Alfred Bester's Gulliver Foyle, the "Common Man" hero of *The Stars My Destination* (1956) learns to "Jaunte"—transport himself instantaneously through space by mental power alone—not by force of will, but by force of hate: he just wants to get away from somewhere that badly. That he succeeds is clearly, again, a matter of chance, but the story built on that chance surely has wide appeal for adolescents chaffing under the parental yoke.

Although such stipulated qualities as brains and passion sometimes offer a thin explanation for the protagonist's special role, often his centrality is justified almost exclusively by chance. E. E. "Doc" Smith's Lensmen series is based on the notion that a superior race gives selected sentients, including human Kimball Kinnison, a "ruby lens" to magnify their mental powers in the service of universal goodness. Shades of Dorothy and the ruby slippers! Billy Pilgrim's travels to Tralfamadore in Kurt Vonnegut, Jr.'s *Slaughterhouse-Five* (1969) occur by the whim of the Tralfamadoreans. And in many novels such as some of those of Arthur C. Clarke (for example, *Childhood's End*, 1953, and *2001*, 1968), the whole human race is serendipitously helped by chance encounters with powers beyond us. This sort of central position is found not only in fairy tales and in science fictions but, for some at least, in the Bible as well.

Of the many motifs made vivid by the Bible, one that functions equally strongly in both fairy tales and science fiction, is that of talking animals. Modern ethology shows us that many animals exhibit traits quite contrary to those assigned them by literature. Male lions, for example, are less "noble" than lazy; pigs are not quite so slovenly as we have portrayed them, and considerably smarter. Nonetheless, animals have been assigned characteristics by fairy tales (and legends and fables) that seem for literary purposes to define those animals. Science fiction writers, giving us back Adam's innocence, often allow their protagonists communication with animals, especially animals in the guise of aliens—and yet, with all of imagination to choose from, these science-fictional animals are typically just revisions of the fairy tale stereotypes. The use of animals in science fiction warrants a full study in itself, but here we can at least sketch in the wide importance of this subject. From the more fantastical side, we find Abraham Merritt's "The Fox Woman" (1946) and wer-creatures of all types, each exhibiting its stereotypical nature: the fox woman comes and goes noiselessly and independently, werwolves are rapacious loners, werdogs fawn on humans. The classic catalog of these oddities is H. G. Wells's *The Island of Dr. Moreau* (1896). Cordwainer Smith has created a whole universe of talking animals with his "Underpeople," such characters as B'dikkat (in "A Planet Called Shayol," 1961), who is made surgically from a bull and who has "brown, cowlike eyes" and pure friendliness, or C'mell (in "The Ballad of Lost C'mell," 1962) who, made surgically from a cat, is slinky, sexy, sensuous, and fundamentally independent despite her existence as a member of a second-class, dependent people. Other cat stereotypes show forth in Larry Niven's fierce, tigerlike race of kzinti (for example, in *Ringworld,* 1972), each an independent warrior who would rather fight to the death than sit back for a moment and think; and in Fritz Leiber's quick-reflexed, sensual and disdainful female alien called Tigerishka (in *The Wanderer,* 1964). Dog creatures, no matter how smart they may be or how they arise, are usually notable primarily for their comforting devotion to human beings, as is true of the title character in Olaf Stapledon's *Sirius* (1944), Sigmund the "mutie Shepherd" in Roger Zelazny's *The Dream Master* (1966), and the protagonist's truest life companion in Harlan Ellison's "A Boy and His Dog" (1969). Despite its apparent freedom to invent, science fiction habitually reuses motifs in their standard forms. A rare addition to the arsenal is James Blish's talking paramecia in "Surface Tension" (1952), but in this world of microscopically small humans, the comparatively large paras, browsing as they do on algae, take on the bovine characteristics of Cordwainer Smith's B'dikkat. And the lion in Arthur C. Clarke's *The Lion of Comarre* (1949), despite the fact that he is called a "superlion," has precisely the same function as the title beast in Aulus Gellius' "Androcles and the Lion" (c. 175

A.D.) If fairy tales and science fictions serve—at admittedly different stages of life—similar needs, we would expect to find similar motifs, and so we do.

Fairy tales have lasted through the ages not because they are familiar, but have become familiar because they have lasted. If fairy tales did not fulfill a continuing need, they would have been forgotten, especially before their collection in the nineteenth century, within a single generation. If science fiction is not original in learning from fairy tales, if its futurism seems less important against this cultural backdrop, we may still retrieve science fiction quite sensibly by recognizing that it deals with the timeless; whether of the past or future is, as Hawthorne said, "of no moment."

Clarke provides us handily with but one of countless examples of powerful science fiction based on older literary and cultural forms. *The Lion of Comarre* is the first of a number of his books in which the hero must break down the separation between a self-contained city and a more pastoral area surrounding it. In this novel the dwellers in the city are lulled by artificially created dreams fed them through surgical connections with their nerves. Clarke uses the term "Lotus Eaters," reminding us of Homer and Tennyson perhaps; his surgical motif had already been used by Fletcher Pratt and Laurence Manning in "City of the Living Dead" (1930). This pleasure-dome image of the dangerously deadening allurements of technology and self-indulgence is worked out again by Clarke in the story "Patent Pending" (1954) and by Shepherd Mead in the satiric novel *The Big Ball of Wax* (1954). The protagonist of *The Lion of Comarre* has a typically central position, "no longer a man, but a symbol, one of the keys to the future of the world."[24] His solution to the stagnation of Comarre rests on the active egocentrism we associate with the immature, a perfect carelessness that the Gallant Tailor would approve: "First he would disconnect the circuits, then he would sabotage the projectors so that they could never again be used. The spell that Comarre had cast over so many minds would be broken forever."[25] Although he does need some help from the superlion he had earlier fed, Richard Peyton III manages to save the world.

Clarke's most notable later versions of this story are *Against the Fall of Night* (1953) and its revision, *The City and the Stars* (1956). The latter begins with this description so clearly dependent upon the style we have seen associated with fairy tales:

> Like a glowing jewel, the city lay upon the breast of the desert. Once it had known change and alteration, but now

Time passed it by. Night and day fled across the desert's face, but in the streets of Diaspar it was always afternoon, and darkness never came. The long winter nights might dust the desert with frost, as the last moisture left in the thin air of Earth congealed—but the city knew neither heat nor cold. It had no contact with the outer world; it was a universe itself.[26]

The city of Diaspar, like the castle of "Sleeping Beauty," hovers in the near-dead "always afternoon." A world sealed off from the wider world, the city awaits renewed contact. Just as the enchanted castle existed "long, long ago," Diaspar exists in that far future when the very atmosphere of Earth has thinned. "Sleeping Beauty" is a story about a girl who at fifteen pricks her finger on a spindle and swoons back into a bed, not to awaken until kissed by her proper mate one hundred years later. The whole of her world falls asleep with her. In Clarke's novel the hero, Alvin, occupies a similarly central position: through no fault of his own he is, as it says in *Against the Fall of Night,* "the only child to be born . . . for seven thousand years."[27] To make this point clearer, the later *The City and the Stars* calls Alvin "the first child to be born . . . for at least ten million years."[28] "Sleeping Beauty" defines its own happy ending as the reawakening of the Princess and her marriage to the Prince; Clarke's novels define their happy endings as the release of the people of the city and the people of the country from their respective isolation. Alvin, like the sexually successful Prince, is the agent of this change: he must break out of the city and into the country to cross-fertilize the cultures and start progress up again. As in the fairy tale, the ending is happy.

If so scientific a man as the inventor of communication satellites could write, and rewrite, a story that fundamentally retells a fairy tale, this does not lessen the importance of the novels, but rather shows that the source of their appeal is in the ageless concerns of people. Fairy tales, like science fictions, begin by hurling us into a world quite different from our own, but then, unlike the chaos of true Fantasies such as *Alice in Wonderland,* fairyland and science fictionland remain stable. The literary journey is accomplished in a moment in order to make available to us—to that audience with special needs—a form in which a supremely important protagonist can take action in a clear and symbolic landscape, action that will give fresh meaning to comfortable conventions and deal with our deepest fears. Near the end of Gregory Benford's *In the Ocean of Night* (1977), Nigel Walmsley—who has received the knowledge that may transform humanity—needs to distract a thug. He says to him, ''I think you're in the wrong fairy tale,'' and so astounds him that Nigel's counterattack is successful.[29] Nigel is right: just as fairy tales are starting points for science fiction, so the fairy tale of traditional science fiction is a starting point for yet newer ways of coming to deal with our lives. Stainislaw Lem understood this when he closed his collection called *The Cyberiad* (1967) with a parodic fairy tale about robots called ''Prince Ferrix and the Princess Crystal.'' His narrator ends his tale by reflecting upon it:

> Well, perhaps it was just another empty invention—there are certainly fables enough in this world. And yet, even if the story isn't true, it does have a grain of sense and instruction to it, and it's entertaining as well, so it's worth the telling.[30]

Both the fables called fairy tales and those modern descendents of them called science fiction, because they deal with the persistent problems of humankind, are worth not only the telling but the reading, too.

Science Fiction
as Truncated Epic

Patrick Parrinder

Far from being settled long ago, the questions of the definition of science fiction and of its relation to other literary forms remain controversial and confused. Perhaps the earliest of the academic literary theorists to have taken notice of science fiction was Northrop Frye, who categorized it in *Anatomy of Criticism* (1957) as a mode of romance.[1] More recently critics have sought a definition that would yield an account of the genre's relationship to science; Darko Suvin's view of it as a "literature of cognitive estrangement" is a much-discussed example.[2] My premise in this essay is that science fiction, like the novel itself, is a typically modern literary form both in its self-consciousness about generic matters and in its evasion of any simple generic definition. Thus I shall not argue that all science fiction is or should be epic, but rather that a number of familiar science fiction texts are significantly related to the epic form. The same texts—not to mention other science fiction works—may also be related to certain of the other traditional forms such as romance, fable, and parody. That is, the traditional generic categories offer a series of overlapping perspectives that may be combined to make up a composite picture of the science fiction genre. Both fable and parody will be invoked later on in this argument; my starting point is the distinction between the epical and the romantic.

The epic has been defined in modern terms by Ezra Pound as a "poem including history."[3] The inclusion of history marks the contrast between the epic and the romance, since the latter form tends to present an absorbing, coherent, and yet arbitrary vision of the world, which the reader can only enter at the price of a willing surrender to the writer's authority.[4] The desirable (including the deliciously horrifying) takes precedence in romance over what is realistically plausible. The author, in Robert Louis Stevenson's words, sets out to

> satisfy the nameless longings of the reader, and to obey the ideal laws of the day-dream. The right kind of thing should fall out in the right kind of place; the right kind of thing should follow; and not only the characters talk aptly and think naturally, but all the circumstances in a tale answer one to another like notes in music.[5]

While this is an evocation of the romance as an ideal type, hence greatly oversimplified, it would seem that the term "scientific romance" as used for early science fiction is something of a misnomer. Pure scientific romance is to be found in some of Hawthorne's tales, where an exotic twist is given to a doomed love match by the labors of a demonic scientist. This is very different from the science fiction of Wells and Verne. Criticism of the romance tends to stress, not its verisimilitude, but its orchestration of emotional effects, viewing it alternatively as a recapturing of some archetypal essence and as a machine for the production of literary pleasure. Yet the solemnity that the myth critic and the structuralist—and even, for that matter, the "aesthetic" critic such as Stevenson—bring to the romance is far from being endemic to this most purely diverting of narrative forms.[6]

The purpose of epic writing is never simply to hold its audience spellbound. The dignity and seriousness of the classical *epos* reflect the fact that the heroic deeds it recounts are supposed to have really taken place, whereas the secondary epics of Dante and Milton lay claim to a profound religious and symbolic truth. Where the romance may be written in a whimsical and parodic manner, drawing attention to the imaginary nature of the world it depicts, epic writing postulates a historical or eschatological continuity between the events it narrates and the reader's situation. These events have both a specified time and place in the historical world, and a permanent national or religious significance for the social group to whom the epic belongs. And although the intervention of gods and goddesses in human affairs is a regular feature of traditional epic, this is portrayed in terms of recognizably human motivations of pity, affection, benevolence, jealousy, and spitefulness rather than as part of an undifferentiated supernatural. The epic is thus a secular or historical narrative of events and deeds that constitute the heritage, or provide the key to the destiny, of the people for whom it is written.

A debased use of the term "epic" is a commonplace of the promotional material on science fiction put out by publishers and film companies. It may, indeed, be the mindless reiteration of the term on paperback covers and movie posters that has led to its comparative neglect by critics of the genre. "Epic" science fiction in the commercial sense invariably involves space travel, since space is the last natural frontier and thus the appropriate setting for a new heroic age of exploration, adventure, and imaginary wars. The story of how the Earth, or some other homeland, was saved is a plausible substitute for the old national epic, concerned with the establishment and defense of the realm. Nevertheless, the run-of-the-mill space epic is usually decked out with the stock figures and situations of conventional romance: villainous monsters, enchanted landscapes, plucky young heroes, and princesses born to send brave men to their deaths. The new heroic age of exploration repeats the discovery of America (we may even end up on a beach with the ruins of the Statue of Liberty, as in the film of Pierre Boulle's *Planet of the Apes*), and the story of how the Earth was saved turns into a cosmic game of cops and robbers or a rerun of World War II. The presence of detailed technical descriptions may help to give the impression of verisimilitude, and thus of a genuine approximation to epic form. The hard technology of *2001: A Space Odyssey* might be compared to Homer's itemization of military equipment, and the purely decorative spacecraft of *Star Wars* are reminiscent of the horses and armor of chivalric romance. However, the principal ground for calling some science fiction "epic" as opposed to "romantic" is that it deals with future or alternative history. The plausibility such stories share with realism is as essential as the heroic deeds and fateful contests they share with modern fantasy.

The events portrayed in epic fiction must be of a certain magnitude. Though they need not be noble deeds in the old sense, they must involve the fate, not of individuals, but of whole societies or of the human race, its collaterals or descendants. Science fiction is often closer than realistic fiction to the old epics by virtue of its universal scale, the scope it allows for heroic enterprise, and its concern with man's confrontation with nonempirical and extraterrestrial forces. Nevertheless, science fiction that takes the form of a fictive history has often been likened to realism.[7] Robert A. Heinlein once tried to define science fiction as a whole as "realistic future-scene fiction."[8] H. G. Wells suggested that the "futurist story . . .

should produce the effect of an historical novel the other way round."[9] He was referring to the illusion of reality it ought to sustain. Though both are related to traditional epic, the idea that the future history and the historical novel are mirror images of one another is to some extent a chronological illusion. Bad historical novels and bad science fiction tend to resemble one another, since both rely on the stereotypes of the romance genres; the essential difference, however, between the fictional bringing-to-life of a past world and the invention of a future one is the difference between historiography and speculation or prophecy.

The great Marxist critic Georg Lukács follows Hegel in arguing that all the modes of modern realism are descendants of the ancient epic. The progressive alienation of man from his fellow men since the dawn of Greek civilization accounts, in his view, for the passing away of the primitive epic form with its direct expression of the "extensive totality of life." The bourgeois novel attempts to recapture the unity of Homer's "rounded universe" through its portrayal of the social trajectory of the "problematic hero."[10] In *The Historical Novel* Lukács argues that the novelists whom he calls "critical realists" are able to evoke the process of social development by means of their portrayal of conflict between typical individuals. (The concept of characters as representative types, it should be noted, is a modern innovation that implies a combination of the epic form with allegory or fable.) The pioneer of the modern realist epic, in Lukács's view, is Sir Walter Scott. Lukács's key distinction between the classical form of Scott's historical novels and the naturalistic costume drama exemplified by Flaubert's *Salammbô* is helpful in considering the nature of science fiction's historical narratives. Scott's novels, according to Lukács, have as their underlying theme the social transformations that have led to the emergence of modern Britain. He shows these historical crises as they were experienced within the being of the age—the broad sweep of everyday life. The conflicts undergone by Scott's middle-of-the-road heroes are those that, in retrospect, may be seen as constituting a decisive parting of the ways in national development. These conflicts are portrayed with a degree of necessary anachronism, since Scott allows his characters to express "feelings and thoughts about real, historical relationships in a much clearer way than the actual men and women of the time could have done."[11] In this way the period in which the novel is set is revealed as part of an essential history leading up to the present.

Flaubert in *Salammbô* portrays a society (that of ancient Carthage in conflict with the Barbarians) that has no organic connection with his own. His novel expresses a "scientific" attitude in its reliance upon historical and archaeological research and in its elimination of any sort of anachronistic historical awareness on the part of its characters. The attractions of *Salammbô* for the reader lie simply in its exoticism and in what Lukács calls its "pseudo-monumentality." However, the exoticism is only superficial, since the emotional conflicts of the protagonists are characterized by an implicit modernization:

> Artists have admired the accomplishment of Flaubert's descriptions. But the effect of Salammbô herself was to provide a heightened image, a decorative symbol, of the hysterical longings and torments of middle-class girls in large cities. History simply provided a decorative, monumental setting for this hysteria, which in the present spends itself in petty and ugly scenes, and which thus acquired a tragic aura quite out of keeping with its real character.[12]

The mode that Lukács is describing here is that of the historical costume drama, in which characters in alien settings and exotic dress are shown pursuing desires of a basically familiar and conventional kind. The pseudomonumentality that Lukács detects is all too familiar in "historical" science fiction, whether the futures it depicts are embodiments of glittering rationality or of neofeudal brutality and splendor. Indeed, the great majority of really lengthy science fiction novels and so-called epics are costume dramas of considerable banality.

Is there, however, a classical form of epic science fiction comparable to that which Lukács discovered in the historical novel? Since there are no credible equivalents to the Waverley novels or *War and Peace,* it has sometimes been suggested that the great epic of science fiction has yet to be written.[13] Yet it must be remembered that future histories differ profoundly from the historical novels of the nineteenth century in that their basis is not history but speculation or prophecy. The concepts of speculation and prophecy require some clarification at this point.

In our secularized societies the idea of prophecy has declined from an article of faith to a strong but residual metaphor. The social prophet is recognizable as such partly by his Old Testament literary manner (as with the so-called Victorian sages) and partly by his concern to direct readers' attention to the future and to anticipate social and technological innovations. Even the most visionary of modern thinkers are prophets only by metaphorical courtesy. Nevertheless, modern society combines scepticism about the possibilities of foretelling with a great hunger for intimations of what the future will hold. Science fiction authors of future histories very frequently gain a reputation as prophets. Conversely, any secular attempt to speculate about the future is a hypothetical exercise and may, if we wish, be described as fictional.

The science fiction that I shall call "prophetic" invokes the authority of the modern cognitive sciences for its speculations about the far future. (We are not concerned here with Jules Verne–like speculations about the very *near* future, in which the vast majority of social data remain unchanged.) The major problem of this mode of writing—one identified by Wells in his remarks about the futurist story—is that while the future history may be convincing in outline, it is very difficult to keep it convincing in detail. The greater the wealth of fictional incident, the greater the reader's awareness is likely to be that he is faced not with logical necessity but with hypothetical and, often, gratuitous fantasy. For this reason, science fiction writers have good reason for sheering away from traditional epic construction in their narratives of the future. The characteristic relationship of many science fiction stories to the older epics is, it would seem, one of truncation or frustration. If the events that they portray are of epic magnitude, the manner of their portrayal is brief and allegorical, reminiscent not of the poem in twelve books but of the traditional fable.

A major example of the truncated epic in science fiction is Wells' *Time Machine,* the story of a voyage of thirty million years into the future that is told in little over 30,000 words. The (unnamed) Time Traveller, a representative nineteenth-century scientist and inventor, comes, as he tells us, "out of this age of ours, this ripe prime of the human race, when Fear does not paralyse and mystery has lost its terrors."[14] He embarks on a Promethean mission, since, from the viewpoint of post-Darwinian evolutionism, knowledge of the future could transform man's sense of the meaning and possibilities of his existence. Wells does not disappoint us in his promise to give a comprehensive and prophetic account of the future. It might be objected that his brevity in doing so was determined by the publishing conditions of the 1890s, but in fact Wells was exploiting a newly won freedom to publish short fiction rather than being forced to confine himself to a certain length. The prospect of *The Time Ma-*

chine in three volumes did not appeal to its author and does not appeal to the reader.[15]

The reason for this brevity lies not only in Wells' didactic intentions, but also in the nature of the scientific thought on which the story is based. The plausibility of *The Time Machine*'s prophecy of the future is proportional, in large part, to the abstract and inhuman nature of the laws of evolution, thermodynamics, and class struggle invoked by the Time Traveller to explain what he sees. Wells could have invented more episodes to show the various intermediate stages of the future and especially the epoch of man's supremacy—a period that he passes over in virtual silence. In fact, as he revised the story, he actually suppressed at least one episode. The story as it stands has an air of historical inevitability, from which further fanciful invention could only detract.

There are two major prophecies in *The Time Machine:* that of the degeneration of human civilization as represented by the Eloi and the Morlocks, and that of the gradual regression of all life on Earth to the point reached in the final scenes on the beach. The episode of the Eloi and Morlocks, although a demonstration of evolutionary decline, seems to embody a warning of the possible consequences of the greed, complacency, and rigid class divisions of present society. Wells here is satirizing both the society in which he grew up (the "overground" and "underground" races paralleling the rigid stratification of the country house in which his mother was housekeeper) and the effete but prosperous societies that utopians such as William Morris foresaw in the near future. The effect is to make sense of man's possible future, since this future appears as the outcome of social choices made in the present. It may be questioned whether the same logic applies to the final scenes, where the progressive extinction of all higher forms of life as a result of planetary cooling is an unforgettable expression of cosmic pessimism. In theory it is possible for mankind to avoid the fate reserved for life on Earth—by migrating into space—but this possibility is not mentioned in the story. Rather, the vision of implacable biological necessity confronting man fulfills the prophetic intimations that came upon the Time Traveller as he gazed, fascinated, upon the "winged sphinx" at the moment of his entry into the world of 802,701:

A colossal figure, carved apparently in some white stone, loomed indistinctly beyond the rhododendrons through the hazy downpour. But all else in the world was invisible. . . . It chanced that the face was towards me; the sightless eyes seemed to watch me; there was the faint shadow of a smile on its lips. It was greatly weather-worn, and that imparted an unpleasant suggestion of disease. *I stood looking at it for a little space—half a minute, perhaps, or half an hour*. It seemed to advance and to recede as the hail drove before it denser and thinner. At last I tore my eyes from it for a moment, and saw that the hail curtain had worn threadbare, and that the sky was lightening with the promise of the sun.

I looked up again at the crouching white shape, and the full temerity of my voyage came suddenly upon me. What might appear when that hazy curtain was altogether withdrawn? What might not have happened to men? What if cruelty had grown into a common passion? What if in this interval the race had lost its manliness, and had developed into something inhuman, unsympathetic, and overwhelmingly powerful? I might seem some old-world savage animal, only the more dreadful and disgusting for our common likeness—a foul creature to be incontinently slain [my emphases].[16]

It is only after his trancelike examination of the sphinx that the Time Traveller is able to make out any other details of the future world. (It is notable that Wells does not describe him taking his eyes off the sphinx the second time; rather, the whole landscape becomes visible behind and around the sphinx.) The statue of the sphinx is an embodiment of the awesomeness of the prophetic vision, which the Time Traveller himself experiences as "the full temerity of my voyage." His fear of finding himself in the grip of overwhelming power is not realized in the world of 802,701 (in which he appears almost godlike to the Eloi, and is able to meet the Morlocks on more or less equal terms), but in the "Further Vision," where he confronts not the descendants of humanity but the "inhuman, unsympathetic, and overwhelmingly powerful" force of entropy that is bringing about the death of the solar system. The epic quality of the story results not only from its projection of future history but also from the Time Traveller's courage in facing the evidence of mankind's futility and in bringing it back to his hearers. He is committed to observing what lies in store for humanity (although he can do no more than observe it), however appalling that knowledge may be. His personal heroism is finally proved by his readiness to embark on a second journey in time—the one from which he never returns. The ambivalence with which a more ordinary humanity must regard such heroism and such prophecy is implied by the narrator's remarks in the Epilogue:

> He, I know—for the question had been discussed among us long before the Time Machine was made—thought but cheerlessly of the Advancement of Mankind, and saw in the growing pile of civilisation only a foolish heaping that must inevitably fall back upon and destroy its makers in the end. If that is so, it remains for us to live as though it were not so. But to me the future is still black and blank—is a vast ignorance, lit at a few casual places by the memory of his story.[17]

The final phrase is a reminder of the difference between prophecy and historiography and, also, of the tentativeness that afflicts all modern epic writing (whether or not it is science-fictional), since there is always a level at which the hero's deeds seem gratuitously inflated and the narrative is "only a story." The fact is that no artist's vision today can mold his society as inescapably as Homer did his.

The Time Machine, then, is a narrative of heroism and prophecy in which the degree of dramatization exactly corresponds to the authority of the "laws of future history" that it invokes. While it is the element of dramatization that constitutes the difference between science-fictional prophecies and those of "futurology,"[18] it remains true that *The Time Machine* would not exist were it not for the anticipative and eschatological tendencies inherent in the scientific thought of Wells' time. The process of extrapolation from the present into the future reflects the basic promise of science, which is that all things can in principle be known because they are subject to "natural law." Yet it has already been argued that "anticipations" belong in the category of fictions and hypotheses, rather than in that of scientific knowledge. Logically they do not differ from models of the world based on premises admitted to be fantastic, provided that the latter models are self-consistent. The most that can be said of them is, in Isaac Asimov's words, that "sometimes such extrapolations are fairly close to what happens."[19] In addition, our response to them is often a factor in determining whether or not they are close to what happens.

Apart from simple assumptions of the order of "if this goes on," twentieth-century science fiction has two basic rational methods of projecting the future—technological determinism and evolutionism. Technological determinism is the belief that man's future will be transformed by technological innovations whose impact it is possible to predict. Evolutionism is the belief that all life is subject to irreversible change under the operation of natural laws such as the need to adapt to its environment or perish. Predictions based on these two beliefs claim the impersonal authority that comes from viewing the future as a process of natural, rather than man-made, history. Such authority, however tentative its actual foundations, has had an almost irresistible attraction for certain science fiction writers.

The basis of technological forecasting is that man's life will be materially transformed in the future as radically, if not far more radically, than it has been in the past. Evolutionism, however, suggests what must be irreparably lost in this process; whether or not mankind is destined to die out like the great dinosaurs, such prophecies invariably involve fundamental changes in human ecology. These prospects have been explored in a growing literature of scientific anticipation, which received great impetus in the earlier twentieth century both from the work of Wells (in fiction and nonfiction) and from the popular writings of such eminent scientists as J. B. S. Haldane and J. D. Bernal. Haldane's *Daedalus: Or, Science and the Future* (1924) and Bernal's *World, the Flesh and the Devil* (1929) are two seminal works in this tradition. In the present context, Haldane's fictional essay "The Last Judgment" (1927) will serve as a classic example of pure prophecy involving both technological determinism and evolutionism. "The Last Judgment" is an eschatological speculation on "the most probable end of our planet as it might appear to spectators on another."[20] Haldane begins by discussing possible causes of the eventual catastrophe—the sun might become a supernova, a huge meteor might collide with the Earth, or planetary cooling might take place—but he concludes that a man-made disaster is far more likely. The disaster he envisions is an unforeseen, long-term consequence of man's greatest technological triumph—the harnessing of tidal power as an energy source— which brings about prosperity and happiness on Earth. But, as his future historian writes in what now seems a manifestation of high optimism, "it was characteristic of the dwellers on earth that they never looked more than a million years ahead, and the amount of energy available was ridiculously squandered."[21] The eventual result is that the speed of the Earth's rotation begins to diminish, causing unprecedented climatic severity and the extinction of virtually all nonhuman species. Alarmed by these events, a group of humans band together and set off to colonize Venus. Disease, crime, and unhappiness reappear among them, but they also evolve new senses, one of which is a form of telepathy. Their biological development is so fast that the crew of the last projectile to reach Venus are discovered to be incapable of fertile unions with the existing colonists; as a result (and this is typical of the ruthlessness of the new Venusian breed) the latecomers are used for experimental purposes. Meanwhile, the Earth's moon splits up, and some of its fragments strike the mother planet, destroying the remnants of terrestrial humanity. The Venusians prepare to recolonize Earth as well as the remainder of the planets of the solar system, breeding specially equipped races to accomplish each task. Their eventual goal is the conquest of the whole galaxy and then—since the galaxy may not survive for more than eighty million million years—of the furthest limits of the universe. The death of the Earth is a negligible event in this process.

The substance of Haldane's prophecy is that man faces a choice between emigration to other worlds and extinction on Earth. The prospect of galactic imperialism that he introduces at the end of "The Last Judgment"—and that is also present in Bernal and the later Wells—was simultaneously providing an "epic" subject matter for the contributors to Gernsback's and other science fiction magazines. The climax of the Wells–Alexander Korda movie *Things to Come* (1935) is one of many places in which the choice of whether or not to colonize the galaxy is posited as a fundamental parting of the ways in future history:

> PASSWORTHY: My God! Is there never to be an age of happiness? Is there never to be rest?
> CABAL: Rest enough for the individual man. Too much of it and too soon, and we call it death. But for MAN no rest and no ending. He must go on—conquest beyond conquest. This little planet and its winds and ways, and all the laws of mind and matter that restrain him. Then the planets about him, and at last out across immensity to the stars. And when he has conquered all the deeps of space and all the mysteries of time— still he will be beginning.[22]

Today's reader may well be tempted to moralize about the trail of destruction and sheer wastage of natural and human resources that a race spreading throughout the universe and dedicated to overcoming every challenge of the environment seems likely to leave behind it. Yet, in literary terms, one might as well lament the despoliation in the *Iliad*. In the decades before the achievement of space flight, galactic imperialism was both a credible prophecy of man's destiny and an ideal framework for the narratives of heroic conflict and resolution that are the legacy of traditional epic. The result was the proliferation of science-fictional costume drama (space opera) and the attempts by writers such as Olaf Stapledon, Arthur C. Clarke, Isaac Asimov, Robert A. Heinlein, and Walter M. Miller to create a more serious mode of future history.

Stapledon was not a professional novelist in the usual sense, and *Last and First Men* (1930), through all its inordinate length, follows the method of factual historiography. At the same time, it pioneers the projection of a cyclical history, which has become commonplace in more recent science fiction. In *Last and First Men* humanity and its descendants rise and fall no less than thirteen times. As Robert H. Canary points out in his discussion of fictive histories, cyclical theories of history serve to familiarize the future, since they entail the repetition of patterns found in the past.[23] The theme of the rise and fall of civilizations has a powerful appeal to historically minded writers; nevertheless, it deserves to be treated with some suspicion. The idea that civilizations reaching a certain stage *must* go into decline, though widespread in the post-Darwinian period, is a capitulation to antiscientific irrationalism. Though the organic analogy for society is valid for some purposes, a society is not a living organism, any more than it is a factory for producing identical china dolls. The popular future histories based, for example, on Oswald Spengler's *Decline of the West*[24] express the fatalistic attitude that the future will be just like the past, if a bit more exotic—and there will be far, far more of that future—rather than anything proper to scientific speculation.

Cyclical histories such as Asimov's trilogy *Foundation* (1951–53) and Walter M. Miller's *Canticle for Leibowitz* (1959) typically consist of a series of disjointed episodes, each introducing a new set of characters and loosely tied together by an overall theme. In *A Canticle for Leibowitz,* for example, the theme is the Catholic church's survival and preservation of fragments of knowledge through the dark ages that succeed each epoch of scientific development. The novel ends with a second nuclear Armageddon on Earth and the departure of a small group of monks in a spaceship. This closure of the cyclical history at a moment of destruction and possible new beginning is one way of ending such a story. Alternatively, as in Clarke's *Childhood's End* (1953), the story may lead to a final mystical apocalypse. (Even the physicist J. D. Bernal indulges in such an apocalypse when, in his speculative essay *The World, the Flesh and the Devil,* he speaks of humanity's "becoming masses of atoms in space communicating by radiation, and ultimately perhaps resolving itself entirely into light.")[25] Both cyclical repetition and ultimate mysticism are ways of shedding light on the "black and blank" future and serve, in fact, as a means of extending the truncated epic to what writers and publishers may consider a proper length. We have seen that technological determinism and evolutionism appear to speak to us with some certainty about the future, but in terms that are brief and cryptic in the extreme. At most, they suggest a number of crises that humanity is bound to confront in the future while saying very little about the order and combination in which these crises will occur. The actual events are bound to be drastically modified by these contextual factors. I should suggest that these considerations have a bearing on the disappointing thinness of the heavyweight histories (notably, those of Stapledon and Asimov) that have been cited. Conversely, they may also account for the excellence of some of science fiction's short stories. The epic strain in science fiction may be present to its greatest advantage where a single future crisis is portrayed with precision and economy. In stories like Clarke's "Sentinel," Murray Leinster's "First Contact," and Clifford D. Simak's "Huddling Place," the possibilities of a future heroic age of space exploration are examined through the medium of what might be termed "epic fables."

Robert A. Heinlein's early future history series is a sequence of stories and novellas, some of which are merely trivial diversions and some of which present a serious view of future crises. The two culminating stories in the sequence, "Universe" and "Common Sense," despite the banalities of their literary style (they were first published in *Astounding Science Fiction,* 1941), are an effective portrayal of the relapse into barbarism following a mutiny aboard a spaceship on a 500-year voyage to Proxima Centauri. Several generations after the mutiny, a small group of men is able to defy the superstitious tyranny that has been established aboard the ship and to recover the knowledge of the mission's nature and purpose. Though much in these stories (reprinted as *Orphans of the Sky*) will hardly bear rereading, the hero's realization that there is a universe outside the ship and his final landing with his followers on a virgin planet fleetingly capture both the strangeness of seeing things for the first time that is essential to science fiction and the noble simplicity that nineteenth-century critics associated with Homer. Here are the closing paragraphs of "Common Sense":

> The sun had crossed a sizable piece of the sky, enough time had passed for a well-fed man to become hungry—and they were not well fed. Even the women were outside—that had been accomplished by the simple expedient of going back in and pushing them out. They had not ventured away from the side of the Ship, but sat huddled against it. But their menfolk had even learned to walk singly, even in open spaces. Alan thought nothing of strutting a full fifty yards away from the shadow of the Ship, and did so more than once, in full sight of the women.
>
> It was on one such journey that a small animal native to the planet let his curiosity exceed his caution. Alan's knife knocked him over and left him kicking. Alan scurried to the spot, grabbed his fat prize by one leg, and bore it proudly back to Hugh. "Look, Hugh, look! Good eating!"
>
> Hugh looked with approval. His first strange fright of the place had passed and had been replaced with a warm deep feeling, a feeling that he had come at last to his long home. This seemed a good omen.
>
> "Yes," he agreed. "Good eating. From now on, Alan, always Good Eating."[26]

This is, of course, very transparent writing. One could go through it separating the authentic primitivism of a new beginning in human history from the bogus, tribal primitivism of Heinlein's *macho* imagination. In addition, how lucky it is that this unsurveyed planet on which Hugh has made a blind landing just happens to be full of trees and juicy small animals! However, the ridiculous improbability involved is something to which Heinlein carefully draws the reader's attention. He can afford to do so, much as Wells could afford the suggestion that the Time Traveller's adventures were no more than a made-up story. "Common Sense" is a prophetic speculation about man's future that satisfies the epic requirements of realism, universality, heroic enterprise, and confrontation with forces beyond man's control. If "Universe" and "Common Sense" together make up a slim book of little over 120 pages, and if even at this length they contain a good deal of superfluous violent action, this should be taken as evidence that the one aspect of the traditional epic that science fiction does not inherit is its amplitude—except in the forms of romantic costume drama and, as we shall see, parody.

Orphans of the Sky and similar works may be used to exemplify one of the classic modes of science fiction: the truncated epic based on the prospect of galactic imperialism, with its associated themes of leaving Earth, colonizing the planets, and meeting with aliens. It remains to be noted that early twentieth-century optimism about the conquest of the universe has now receded, so that these themes can no longer be successfully treated with the epic simplicity that Heinlein found possible. The urge to write the epitaph of the space age is strong in such influential science fiction writers of the 1960s as Kurt Vonnegut, Jr., J. G. Ballard, and even perhaps Stanislaw Lem. Both Vonnegut in *The Sirens of Titan* and Ballard in many of his short stories offer deliberate parodies of the future history. Ballard's "Thirteen for Centaurus" is a neat reversal of *Orphans of the Sky,* in which a precocious adolescent on board a multigenerational spaceship manages to deduce, not only that there is a world outside the ship, but also that "outside" is not deep space but a psychological laboratory on Earth. The simulated space voyage began as a courageous experiment to provide the necessary data for actual voyages; after two generations, during which public opinion has decisively turned against the space program, it has turned into an embarrassing anachronism. As one of the psychologists monitoring the experiment reflects, "What began as a grand adventure of the spirit of Columbus, has become a grisly joke."[27] The joke is at the expense not only of the brainwashed crew—and of the psychologists who believe that men can be kept in ignorance indefinitely—but also of galactic imperialism as a whole. In this and other stories Ballard deliberately takes the form of the truncated epic and turns it inside out.

When the old epics lost their primary authority over their readers, they gave rise to the various modes of mock epic, comic epic, satire, and burlesque. Lucian's *True History,* the earliest surviving narrative of interplanetary travel, begins as a parody of the *Iliad* and the *Odyssey.* In recent years comic fantasy has become a prominent science-fictional mode; one thinks not only of *The Sirens of Titan* but as well of Calvino's *Cosmicomics* and of the seemingly inexhaustible episodes of Lem's *Cyberiad* and *Star Diaries.* Other recent science fiction shows not so much an inversion of the epic mode as its fusion with different generic elements. The representative science fiction novels of the 1960s and 1970s are, by and large, not future histories but stories of parallel worlds created by changing or simply stepping outside man's actual historical world. Philip K. Dick's *Man in the High Castle* and Kingsley Amis' *Alteration* are well-known examples of this mode, but, at a more complex level, there is Lem's *Solaris,* in which the development of the science of Solaristics is analogous to, rather than being a plausible extension of, present-day scientific thought. *Solaris* is a "novel including history," but the history is that of an alternative future in which the unique and remarkable qualities of a single, remote planet have become a human obsession. The Solaris ocean is a "godlike" being at least to the extent that it makes mysterious interventions in human lives. Epic heroism enters the novel through Kelvin's struggle (which may or may not be successful) to conquer his scientific and emotional immaturity and to carry on the work of his great predecessors in Solaristics. The ending of the novel, in which he at last completes his long voyage from Earth by landing on the surface of the alien planet, is epic both in its dramatization of Kelvin's bold decision to stay on Solaris and in its prophetic intimation that "the time of cruel miracles was not past."[28] Yet, although *Solaris* thus ends with a prophecy, it is one with no more than a distantly analogical relationship to scientific anticipation in the world in which we live.

Science fiction since the end of the 1950s has become more self-conscious, more freely speculative, and more intellectually ambitious. It would be tempting to think that its Homeric primary epics might now give way to secondary epics. Yet I suspect that a more fruitful approach—which I have no space to develop here—would be to examine a contemporary masterpiece such as *Solaris* as an intricate combination of epic, fable, romance, and parody elements. The argument of this essay has been that epic science fiction has arisen where writers have most responded to those scientific anticipations that may be studied in the literature of so-called popular science.[29] Where such anticipations seem likely to affect the whole of man's future—even though they can do no more than to illumine a few casual places in the blackness and blankness of that future—science fiction has responded by dramatizing them in the form of the truncated epic.

Science Fiction and the Gothic

Thomas H. Keeling

Critical histories of science fiction usually link the development of this genre with that of the gothic novel. Tracing the genealogies of modern robots and androids through the labyrinths of gothic nightmare, scholars invariably lead us into Victor Frankenstein's "workshop of filthy creation"; in Hawthorne's "Birthmark" and "Rappaccini's Daughter," they find prototypes of the modern "man of science," the hero-villain of so much science fiction. Similarly, works such as Poe's *Narrative of Arthur Gordon Pym,* Stevenson's *Dr. Jekyll and Mr. Hyde,* and Wells' *Island of Dr. Moreau* frequently find their way into studies of both gothic and science fiction. Contemporary science fiction writers, moreover, appear to be fascinated by the gothic, as illustrated by the success with which Walter Miller, in *A Canticle for Leibowitz,* Ursula Le Guin, in *The Left Hand of Darkness*, and Stanislaw Lem, in *Solaris,* integrate traditional gothic motifs into science fiction narratives.

Recognition of the historical ties and apparent structural similarities that link these two genres has led a number of critics to speak of science fiction as if it were simply an "updated" gothic form that appeals to the same fantasies and expectations as the earlier gothic. Brian Aldiss asserts that science fiction, born of the gothic mode, "is hardly free of it now."[1] Both forms deal in enchantment and nightmare, he suggests, and both employ methods of narrative distancing, the only real difference being that gothicists set their fantasies in the past—usually in the Catholic south—while science fiction writers project their fantasies into future worlds, alien worlds, or alternate worlds. Leslie Fiedler offers the same argument and actually refers to science fiction as a "neogothic" form.[2] For such critics, the themes and motifs of science fiction are merely a futuristic displacement of the gothic: the old sorcerers become the modern physicists; demonic possession becomes telepathic control; corpses, once animated supernaturally, are now rejuvenated with the help of cryogenics; and time travel renders superfluous the elaborate rites once used to conjure up the spirits of the dead.

These suggestive surface-level parallels may be more clearly illustrated in a brief examination of two specific novels, M. G. Lewis's classic eighteenth-century romance *The Monk* and Philip Dick's *Ubik*. Rather than provide lengthy plot summaries of these two works, I shall move quickly to some of the more important structural, conceptual, and aesthetic parallels. Here it is sufficient to observe that *The Monk* is a weave of two tales, the first being that of a Capuchin monk, Ambrosio, whose sexual obsession weakens his resistence to demonic influence, leads him to commit "inhuman" crimes, and eventually precipitates his destruction. The subplot centers on two tormented lovers, Raymond and Agnes; while Raymond fights to free himself from the physical and psychological hold of an ancient specter called the "Bleeding Nun," Agnes endures excruciating torture in the subterranean tombs of a convent. Philip Dick's *Ubik* focuses on the hero's struggle to survive the chaos created by individuals possessing extraordinary psychic abilities and by the curious mental state known as "half-life," which results when people are frozen immediately after death.

The plots of both novels hinge upon the intervention of beings endowed with apparently supernatural powers. As a grisly phantom from Raymond's ancestral past, the Bleeding Nun is clearly a true supernatural, demonic agent, as are the Wandering Jew, whose exorcism frees Raymond, and Matilda, the demonic *femme fatale* who unleashes Ambrosio's suppressed sexual appetite. In *Ubik* the characters' frightening psychic abilities (including telepathy and precognition) result from an advance in human evolution. Jory, the half-lifer who is the ultimate "demon" in this story, seems to be a transformed gothic monster, not only in his strange cannibalism (reminiscent of the vampire's), but also in such physical traits as his pointed teeth and incongruous facial features.

The second and more significant parallel lies in the way these characters use their powers to violate those basic experiential premises we normally take for granted. By penetrating into the minds of others in order to influence their perception and behavior, the Bleeding Nun, Matilda, and Ambrosio all represent a threat to the long-cherished concept of the self as a discrete and inviolable category, just as Jory and the telepaths do in *Ubik*. Moreover, in both novels the violation of self produces temporal and spatial disorientation and an overall sense of what Wolfgang Kayser, speaking of the aesthetics of the grotesque, calls "alienation and estrangement."[3]

This transgression of boundaries normally considered discrete is usually accompanied by physical grotesquerie, which is the third major respect in which *The Monk* and *Ubik* resemble each other. In one of the most graphically grotesque scenes of Lewis' tale, Agnes awakens in darkness, grasps something soft, and advances it toward her: "In spite of its putridity, and the worms which preyed upon it, I perceived a corrupted human head."[4] Starving in a subterranean vault, she later clings tenaciously to the decaying, worm-infested corpse of her own infant. Scarcely less "gothic" are Philip Dick's descriptions of the remains of Jory's victims, dehydrated, almost mummified heaps of bones with leering, paper-like skulls and recessed eyes.[5]

These glances at *The Monk* and *Ubik* underscore the fact that gothic and science fiction may also share a common reader appeal. It does not follow from these observations, however, that science fiction is simply a neogothic form—that aside from the substitution of a fear of the future for a fear of the past, the narrative "formula" is essentially the same in both genres. Science fiction is not, in fact, an updated and disguised form of gothicism. In order to isolate the actual generic differences that separate gothic and science fiction, we must penetrate beyond the observable surface-level types and paraphernalia—the relentless and mysterious villains, the deranged scientists, the haunted castles, the starships, the ray guns, and the trap doors. They, after all, are but the "signs" by which we recognize these genres; they recur only because they are among the necessary correlates of other, deeper structures or because they most readily and convincingly image forth those underlying laws and conditions that truly define the fictional worlds of gothic and science fiction. If we are indeed looking at two distinct genres, then on the level of structural and aesthetic premises we expect to find some essential differences beneath the many suggestive but finally accidental similarities.

I. The first constant in the generic paradigm that defines the older genre, the gothic novel, is the presence of one or more "demonic agents," characters whose obsession (or "possession") radically restricts their vision and behavior, giving them the appearance of being driven by forces alien and external to them.[6] Demonic agents may be possessed by a certain "ruling passion" (lust, in the case of Ambrosio) or by a particular belief or image that becomes an *idée fixe* (as in the cases of Victor Frankenstein and Hawthorne's Aylmer). Of course, they may also be possessed by actual supernatural forces; for example, Ambrosio's psychological obsessions facilitate actual "possession" by the demon, Matilda, and eventually by Lucifer himself. Natural and supernatural types of possession function simultaneously in *The Monk* and in most other major gothic novels to produce a pattern of behavior that may be human in kind, but that is demonic in intensity and force.

Like St. Anthony and other ascetics, the demonic agent tends to generate his world around him. Action and setting are therefore largely the exteriorization of internal nightmare and obsession. Schedoni's shadowy machinations in Mrs. Radcliffe's *Italian* reveal more about the obsessed mind of Ellena, the heroine through whose fears we experience the events of the novel, than about Schedoni himself. Indeed, to the extent that the persecuted maiden creates the gothic villain out of her subconscious fears and desires, she is her own persecutor. So too, the nightmarish *Doppelgänger* of gothic fiction usually originates in the hidden recesses of the demonic agent's psyche. The images of decay, the haunted—seemingly animistic—landscapes, and the labyrinthine systems of vaults and passageways that recur frequently in gothic fiction are, on another level, metaphors revealing the interior landscape of the demonic agent.

Demonic agency *may* occur in any prose genre, including science fiction. (Indeed, Angus Fletcher has even suggested that the perfect agent is not a man possessed by a "daemon," but a robot such as Talus or those in Capek's RUR.)[7] Manipulated by forces completely beyond his comprehension or control, this kind of agent becomes little more than a puppet. In *Ubik* we happen to have a kind of demonic agent in the character of Jory, who is actually described as a monster in his attack on Joe Chips, the hero, and who is quite capable of engulfing others in a strange, projected world of his own.

However, demonic agency is not an essential element in science fiction, as it is in the gothic paradigm. The fictional world projected in science fiction, unlike that of the gothic, is not necessarily the revelation of hidden fear, nightmare, or supernatural force; more often it is the visual analogue for a configuration of abstract, philosophical ideas or an extrapolation based upon a given system or condition. In Le Guin's *Dispossessed,* for example, the model established with the contrasting worlds of Urras and Anarres reflects contrasting political, social, and philosophical points of view.

Shevek, whose purpose is to reunite these two cultures, never approaches the inflexible, monomaniacal archetype of the demonic agent. Nor do we find demonic agency as a controlling vision or narrative device in works such as Larry Niven's *Ringworld* or Philip Dick's *Man in the High Castle,* where the focus is again on a particular matrix of ideas rather than on the expression of a single obsessed or possessed psyche.

When possession does occur in science fiction, moreover, it is frequently only a narrative device or embellishment. Consider Stapledon's *Last and First Men,* in which the speaker is a disembodied intelligence of the distant future who has "possessed," or "inspired," the twentieth-century man who is writing the narrative. Significantly, the novel does not focus on this possession at all; Stapledon refers to it as a "device": "only by some such trick could I do justice to the conviction that our whole present mentality is but a confused and halting first experiment."[8] "Mentality" here refers to that of the race or culture, for Stapledon's aim is "myth" in the cultural sense—not the exploration of an individual psyche. When such possession occurs in the gothic, as it does in Hogg's *Confessions* and in the Bleeding Nun episode of *The Monk,* it becomes the actual subject or focus rather than a "device" in Stapledon's sense. Demonic agency, an essential element of the gothic, is merely an accidental feature in science fiction, not one of the genre's structural prerequisites.

II. The gothic universe in which agents function is pandeterministic, and pandeterminism is the second constant in gothic fiction. In its most abstract sense, pandeterminism signifies that "the limit between the physical and the mental, between matter and spirit, between word and thing, ceases to be impervious."[9] Pandeterminism implies an unseen causal system in which relations exist on all levels, thus subverting our normal expectations of cause and effect; it is this aspect of the gothic that we call the "supernatural." A pandeterministic world is one in which the categories of experience that we regard as discrete (self and not-self, dream and reality, animate and inanimate, human and animal, and so on) become penetrable, their boundaries vulnerable to transgression. In such a world all causes and, therefore, all events, are related to one another by strict laws that are never fully revealed. The corollary to pandeterminism is thus pansignification; since relations exist on all levels, among all elements of the world, this world becomes highly significant—everything is charged with meaning: a blood-stained dagger, a lost manuscript, an offhand allusion to an heir presumed dead, a physiognomical resemblance—all details are significant and somehow related to one another.

In the gothic novel pandeterminism means that the relations between events defy both human logic and empirical cause and effect. We may "feel" as if events were linked by some divine or infernal logic, but this causation is beyond the laws of nature and altogether unknowable. No advance in physics or parapsychology will "explain" Lorenzo's prophetic dream, in which he sees Antonia ravished and destroyed by an enormous fire-breathing form. We cannot cite a new discovery in geriatrics to explain the mystery of the Wandering Jew, nor can we explain in empirical or psychological terms how his bizarre exorcism succeeds in ridding Raymond of the curse of the Bleeding Nun. The sciences of statistics and probability theory, even if they were perfected, could not account for the incredible series of coincidences that toss Raymond into the skeletal arms of the Bleeding Nun, who, as it turns out, is really the ghost of his grandfather's great-aunt. Nor could they explain why, of all the girls in the world, Antonia should be the one Ambrosio torments, rapes, and murders; Antonia, we discover, is really Ambrosio's sister, a fact that Lucifer reveals to Ambrosio in the final pages of the novel. We may, of course, discover the psychological or ethical "meaning" of such relations and patterns of causation, but the "how" remains mysterious and unknowable by definition. The violations and transgressions occur or appear to occur in outright defiance of our empirically determined experiential categories, without any pretension that they can be rationally understood.

Causation of this sort has no real place in science fiction, though it often seems to. In science fiction, as in the gothic, the categories of time and space are violated constantly. Wells' hero does so by means of a time machine, rocket commandos of space opera freely teleport themselves throughout the universe, and in *The Sirens of Titan* a strange "Chronosynclastic Infundibula" results in amazing leaps through time and space. Clearly, many of these "miracles" are no less implausible than Ambrosio's magic myrtle or his demon-assisted escape from the dungeons of the Inquisiton. In order to distinguish action and causation in the gothic from action and causation in science fiction, we must look not to the events themselves—for they are equally fabulous—but to the rhetoric employed to account for these events.

Even in Anne Radcliffe's so-called Explained Supernatural, the aesthetics of terror (always related to the sublime and the grotesque) depend upon the impression that the natural laws and categories have been suspended—that dark, demonic forces have intruded into the natural world. Science fiction, on the other hand, relies upon the premise that all events—no matter how fantastic—have natural, that is, empirical or "scientific" causes. Consider the apparent pandeterminism of *Ubik,* where Philip Dick rivals any gothicist in his violations of the categories of time and self. Pat Conley's "talent" enables her not only to see alternate futures, "laid out side by side like cells in a beehive," but actually to change the past and, therefore, the present according to her needs or her whims. That her victim may be shifted from one existence to another without ever knowing it is a kind of violation far more radical than Matilda's manipulation of Ambrosio. Yet Dick demands that his readers accept the acquisition of such amazing talents and antitalents as a natural step in the evolution of the species.

Futhermore, the temporal disorientation experienced by Joe Chips is even more frightening than the demonic penetration of the past into the present that we find in the Bleeding Nun episode of *The Monk;* it is actually a deterioration of the present into archaic forms—a massive assault on the entire fabric of our physical and psychological existence. Yet neither Joe nor the reader is ever tempted to assume supernatural causation; the causes may be unknown, but they are not altogether beyond science. We soon discover that much of what Joe experiences is the result of his being in half-life and of being subjected to Jory's unusual powers. Even when there is no satisfying answer whatsoever—as in Lem's *Solaris* and *The Investigation,* both novels concerned with the process of seeking answers to the unanswerable—we are not invited to conclude that causation is supernatural, only that our mental sets are inadequate, finally insufficient in dealing with the cosmos. In spite of many provocative but accidental similarities between the events in gothic and science fiction, the two genres differ in their essential causal premises.

III. The third constant in gothic fiction concerns the moral axis, the ethical perspective that the genre accepts, either implicitly or explicitly. Whatever is perceived as "alien" here—whatever seems to intrude into the otherwise stable and usually bourgeois world—is always perceived as "evil" as well. Behind demonic agency, behind gothic pandeterminism, and behind the grotesqueries of the gothic landscape, we inevitably encounter a vertical, dualistic, Manichaean world view, which, regardless of how complex the psychology or aesthetics may be, ultimately resolves the conflict in terms of good and evil. Obviously true of *The Castle of Otranto,* Radcliffe's romances, and *The Monk,* it is also true of such complex works as *The Turn of the Screw* and *Absalom, Absalom!,* where the old demons have been transformed and internalized or have retreated into the landscape.

This moral perspective has no necessary place in science fiction, however, where schisms are more likely to develop between the sterile and the generative, human logic and alien logic, "nature" and "science," man and science, or between contrasting socioeconomic and cultural systems rather than between absolute good and evil. Where would we locate absolute good and absolute evil in *The Dispossessed?* Though Le Guin cannot conceal implicit judgments regarding the relative merits of the cultures of Urras and Anarres, those judgments cannot be expressed in absolute moral terms. The interest in alternate worlds in Philip Dick's *Man in the High Castle* is speculative rather than normative, and man's urge to explain and evaluate reality in moral terms is effectively parodied in such works as *The War of the Worlds, The Sirens of Titan,* and *The Investigation,* where chance, evolution, Brownian motion, and whimsy replace the Christian moral order so essential to the gothic. Even in *Ubik,* where Pat Conley and Jory appear almost demonic at times, the conflicts between the Psis and the Norms and between Jory and the other half-lifers are formulated in terms of survival and adaptation rather than in terms of absolute good and evil.

The "evil" alien in gothic fiction is a form of chaos that disrupts the "good" and stable norm. Indeed, the plots of almost all early gothic romances, including *The Monk,* progress toward the restoration of order. The element of chaos (evil), although it is usually manifested in supernatural agency and causation and grotesque imagery, is almost invariably historical or psychological in origin. It threatens always to destroy or transform the positive norm, which is generally bourgeois in values and expectations. Chastity and "virtuous" love and marriage, cleanliness, financial security, the family, Christian ethics, and a kind of psychological sanctity and common-sense hold on reality—these are the values the gothicist must defend, however insincerely or ineffectively. Essentially conservative in its fear of the past, its fear of subconscious desires (a fear ironically at odds with the genre's effects and techniques), and its fear of innovations that might breed chaos, gothic fiction is an ideal form for the exploration of different psychological states and aesthetic points of view. However, its underlying values and perspectives generally render it useless as a vehicle for treating larger systems or problems of a sociological, economic, political, scientific, or philosophical nature.

If the gothic is a fundamentally conservative genre in this respect, science fiction can be viewed as potentially "subversive" insofar as it is not restricted to a moral vision of the world, and certainly not to a conventional Christian interpretation of reality. Furthermore, the science fiction writer, unlike the gothicist, has no necessary commitment to bourgeois reality as it is. In fact, the disrupting alien elements may actually be seen as part of an inevitable and desirable change. In Sturgeon's *More Than Human* and in Clarke's *Childhood's End*, for example, the emergence of "Homo Gestalt," supplanting "normal" humanity, represents a greater perfection of the species. The gothicist would regard Homo Gestalt as a physical and moral threat to the accepted norm, a manifestation of something indisputably evil. Lester del Rey asks that his Homo Mechanensis, "Helen O'Loy," be accepted as an "ideal" woman; for the gothicist, on the other hand, automata, puppets, and doubles figure among the most grotesque and threatening of all demonic creations.

Of course, the science fiction writer may adhere strictly to a good-versus-evil, hero-versus-villain moral perspective. This frequently results in futuristic "Cowboys and Indians" à la *Battlestar Galactica*. Where the absolute moral vision survives untransformed and unassailed in science fiction, we are not surprised to find ourselves trudging through naïve alien-invasion stories of the comic-book variety or space opera of the sort Harry Harrison parodies in "Space Rats of the CCC." In most serious works of science fiction, labeling the alien element "good" or "evil" would run counter to the authors' intentions. It is essential to Le Guin's purposes in *The Left Hand of Darkness* that Genly Ai, our "normal" persona, eventually understand and accept the strangely androgynous Gethenian, Estraven, for this study of an alien sexuality is really a study in the psychology and sociology of human sexuality. The gothicist, of course, would see Estraven as a grotesque bisexual, a living affront to the all-important categories of male and female. Indeed, the confusion of masculinity and femininity in Lewis' Matilda—who is at one point the vaguely homosexual boy, Rosario—is one of the demon's most grotesque characteristics, a point that disturbs even Ambrosio.

Le Guin's fiction is subversive, not because of any reversal of moral polarities, but because the conventional moral axis becomes either an idea to be studied or an altogether irrelevant archaism. The elaborate future history of our species in Stapledon's *Last and First Men* treats as petty or genuinely foolish some of our most sacred cultural assumptions; it too is a subversive novel when compared to the gothicists' defenses of those assumptions. Philip Dick's *Man in the High Castle* challenges our rarely questioned assumptions regarding our desirable victory over the "evil" Japanese in World War II; *Ubik* obliterates, without apology, the distinctions between life and death and between self and not-self around which so much of our world view is oriented. These novels are analytical, speculative, and subversive at precisely those critical points at which a gothicist would have to be judgmental, didactic, and conservative.

In summary, then, the three *essential* elements of the gothic's generic paradigm—demonic agency, pandeterministic causation, and a clear Manichaean moral perspective—are, at best, accidental characteristics of science fiction. Pandeterminism, in fact, is actually incompatible with science fiction's conceptual and rhetorical premises. The gothic novel is an ideal form for the exploration of individual psychology, especially aberrant psychology, as well as of aesthetic concepts such as the sublime and the grotesque. However, the same structural elements that define the genre and that make gothic fiction such an effective means of examining the interior landscape also limit the genre, making it generally inadequate as a means of social criticism or of cultural, political, philosophical, or scientific speculation. These, of course, are the areas in which science fiction excels. Unhampered by the gothic's necessary moral perspective and unrestricted by its fairly narrow range of narrative assumptions and aesthetic premises, science fiction can move freely through a greater range of subjects and points of view and employ a greater variety of narrative structures than the gothic can.

It is not the purpose of this study to contribute to the proliferation of definitions of science fiction. The generic paradigm I have used in distinguishing between these two genres reveals much more about the gothic than about science fiction. However, any extended discussion of what science fiction is not raises the question of what it is, and several useful lines of definition do seem to have emerged from these comparative observations.

Science fiction's vision extends outward, away from the interior man, exploring instead man's relationship with his natural and artificial environments. In doing so, science fiction shares common ground with political novels, adventure novels, travel narratives, and satirical fantasies such as *Utopia, Gulliver's Travels,* and *A*

Connecticut Yankee in King Arthur's Court. While such concerns in no way preclude close attention to psychological detail, they become secondary to the interplay of ideas on a larger scale. Even when science fiction appears to deal with the interior of a single psyche, its actual focus shifts from the mind *per se* to the mind as it responds to or is modified by some technical or scientific innovation.

If science fiction may be distinguished from the gothic and other confessional forms by its emphasis on "ideas" rather than on the labyrinthine depths of the individual mind, these "ideas" may, in turn, be defined by a specific rhetoric or perspective. Although the miracles of science fiction are frequently as implausible as those of the gothic necromancer, they are premised on a faith that the universe is an essentially "natural" phenomenon, ultimately accessible to the rational or scientific mind. This premise remains true even in works such as *Solaris,* which concludes that the universe is essentially unknowable to man because he is limited by his own perceptual and conceptual sets or lenses. In this respect, Lem's novels resemble Gödel's Theorem and the Heisenberg Principle: both challenge man's ability to arrive at absolute certainty with modern tools, yet they are, in themselves, impressive achievements of the scientific frame of mind and in no way invite prescientific or supernatural alternatives. Lem can arrive at his conclusions only through the literary equivalent of an "experiment": the controlled application of logic and scientific knowledge. This assumption of the validity of scientific reasoning holds also in works such as *A Canticle for Leibowitz* and *Brave New World,* which reflect our deepest fears of science and technology.

Science fiction, then, is a form of fiction that, unlike confessional or psychological fiction, focuses on man's relationship with his natural and man-made environments and that, unlike such works as *The Faerie Queene,* assumes that the scientific perspective—even though it is imperfect and is the frequent cause of our crises—is still our best tool in dealing with those environments. What this formulation lacks is something that would clearly differentiate science fiction from "realistic" novels dealing with man's sociopolitical environment (for example, *La Comédie humaine*) or fiction influenced by Zola's attempted application of scientific methods. Political and social novels examine directly the truth of man's condition as it is or has been in the historical past. Science fiction begins with a "What if?" proposition, locating its speculations in the future, in alien worlds, or in a past modified or reinvented by science. The strategy is one of projection and extrapolation. Its strength lies in the fact that, although it rewards our deepest desires temporarily to escape reality as it is, it finally brings us back to a reexamination of the present.[10] Darko Suvin and others have argued that this "attitude of estrangement" has become essential to the structure of the genre. The projected setting becomes a displaced image of the present, a mirror that, as Suvin observes, both reflects and transforms the world as we know it.[11] The "sense of wonder" so often associated with science fiction originates in this strategy of displacement and extrapolation—not in the genre's concern with man and his environment or in its "scientific" premises.

Entertaining for a moment the idea that a genre has an absolute and immutable form, we might attribute to science fiction three primary characteristics: (1) Science fiction is that class of fiction that focuses upon man's relationship with his environment rather than upon individual psychology. (2) It accepts and uses the premises of modern science in its examination of phenomena and in its extrapolations. (3) The genre employs the narrative strategy of displacement or estrangement ("fabulation") in distancing the fiction. This three-part definition of science fiction acknowledges the genre's similarities to other genres at the same time it isolates or distinguishes it. Science fiction and gothic fiction share the third criterion but not the first two. The second criterion is the only one that separates science fiction from allegorical and satirical works such as *The Faerie Queene* and *Gulliver's Travels*. And only the third criterion distinguishes science fiction from much of what we call "realistic" or "naturalistic" fiction.

Of course, generic models should be formulated and applied with caution and humility, for it is easy to forget that taxonomy is not a goal in itself but, rather, a means with which we may better understand a particular type of literature. Moreover, literary genres are not fixed; they blend, disappear, and reemerge as something strange and new. It is possible for science fiction to use the gothic as a "mode," employing the gothic's peculiar atmosphere and psychological orientation for its own purposes. *A Canticle for Leibowitz* and *The Investigation* succeed admirably at this. On the other hand, the strategies of science fiction itself may be subordinated to other forms. C. S. Lewis's trilogy is an elaborate Christian parable that exploits science fiction techniques but that ultimately rejects the premise that the universe is a natural phenomenon approachable through scientific reasoning. Because the conditions under which fiction is written change and because the strongest authors usually modify inherited forms, fictional genres tend to diffuse and become less distinct. While authors today frequently exploit the gothic as a mode or strategem, we must look back almost a century to find a serious novel that is unambiguously "pure" gothic. I suspect that in the next few decades science fiction will undergo similar transformations, becoming more versatile as a mode and less distinct as a genre.

Philip Dick's *Man in the High Castle* and the Nature of Science-Fictional Worlds

Carl D. Malmgren

> Actually, the very existence of narra-
> tive fiction, whatever its content, is an
> indictment of history on esthetic and
> moral grounds.
> Robert Champigny, **The Ontology of**
> **Narrative**

Even a limited exposure to Philip K. Dick's extensive science fiction corpus reveals that two themes with which he is most preoccupied are the creation and function of alternate universes and the subjective nature of reality in a totally relativistic universe.[1] The most well-known Dick texts—*Ubik, Martian Time-Slip, Do Androids Dream of Electric Sheep?, A Maze of Death, The Three Stigmata of Palmer Eldritch*—all deal directly or indirectly with one or both of these themes. Of course, these themes are interconnected, and it is probably *The Man in the High Castle* that most thoroughly explores the nature of that interconnectedness and in so doing throws light on the nature of science fictional worlds and the distinctiveness of science fiction as a narrative subgenre.

Dick seems acutely aware that "reality" can no longer be considered apart from the consciousness that "intends" it, that "reality" is no longer monolithic or objectively given. The ineluctable subjectivity of reality is reflected in Dick's narrative technique; almost never does he provide the reader with a privileged, authorial persona. In the typical Dick fiction, the fictional reality is not presented as existing apart from the characters but is filtered through the medium of their consciousnesses. In *The Man in the High Castle* the narrative unfolds in a number of successive centers of consciousness—Childan, Frank and Juliana Frink, Tagomi, and Baynes. This technique enables Dick to keep track of two relatively separate plot systems (the San Francisco plot and the Rocky Mountain plot, with the Frinks, the I Ching, and *The Grasshopper Lies Heavy* serving as points of connection), but more importantly enacts a fundamental premise of the text—that is, that reality is a subjective affair.

Reality is not only subjective, it is also very elusive and enigmatic. Characters in Dick's fictions frequently find it almost impossible to distinguish between what seems to be happening and what really is happening. They wonder if their perceptions of reality correspond in part or in substance with the "true" current of events; they wonder if there *is* a "true" current of events. In *The Man in the High Castle* this uncertainty manifests itself throughout the text, particularly in the characters' penchant for relying upon the I Ching to discover as it were the "deep structure" of reality, the real and ineluctable current that informs an indeterminate and contingent reality. In Dick's ontology, surfaces are transient and multiple and relative, but there is an essence of truth somewhere beneath the surfaces.

In a world in which relativism and contingency rule the surfaces of experience, it is particularly the province of Art to discover and reveal essences, and Dick's text specifically addresses itself to the relation posited between illusion and reality in any work of art. One of the central motifs in the text consists of meta-artistic speculations about the nature and function of art, and the ending of the novel hinges on the problematics of the Appearance-Reality, Art-Life dichotomies. In various contexts the reader finds references to the truth of the Bible, the value of science fiction novels, the "wu" of Frink's jewelry designs, the intrinsic charm of poetry. Very early in the text Frink meditates on the I Ching's status as a kind of master fiction, a codified body of artistic truth: "A book created by the sages of China over a period of five thousand years, winnowed, perfected, that superb cosmology—and science—codified before Europe had even learned to do long division."[2] The I Ching represents in the novel a work of Art that reveals the reality beneath illusory and often confusing surfaces.

These metatextual references help to identify *The Man in the High Castle* as a text concerned with the role of illusion in Art, specifically with the nature and function of fictionality, a concern that culminates in the role of the novel within the novel—Hawthorne Abendsen's *Grasshopper Lies Heavy*. The instrumentality of this science fictional text within a text reveals Dick as a science fiction metafictionist, concerned with exploring the how and what of science fiction, a motif that culminates in Juliana Frink's visit to the "man in the high castle." Armed with knowledge of the threat to Abendsen's life and an intuitive grasp of the meaning of *The Grasshopper Lies Heavy,* Juliana makes it into Abendsen's house and verifies her feeling that Abendsen wrote the novel by consulting the I Ching. Abendsen's wife reveals that the I Ching is responsible for the entire novel, for subject, characters, plot, setting, and so on. Juliana, in her straightforward fashion, then puts her finger on the real mystery of the situation—the reason for the intervention of I Ching—and insists that they throw coins to discover that reason. The hexagram that results is Chung Fu (Inner Truth), and both Abendsen and Juliana take this message literally:

> Raising his head, Hawthorne scrutinized her. He had now an almost savage expression. "It means, does it, that my book is true?"
> "Yes," she said.
> With anger he said, "Germany and Japan lost the war?"
> "Yes."[3]

Abendsen tends to refuse to accept this incredible fact, but Juliana embraces it. In one bold stroke the characters are informed of their own fictionality and thus the fictionality of this particular realized alternate universe. In the same stroke the novel reveals to the reader its own fictionality, its made-upness, its fraudulence. Juliana feels liberated by this information ("Now I can see there's nothing to be afraid of, nothing to want or hate or avoid, here, or run from."),[4] but how is the reader to respond to Juliana's insouciance, to the abrupt ending, or to the uncomfortable destruction of the fictional illusion?

The ending brings home for the reader the inescapable fact that Dick's primary concern lies less in making this particular fictional world pertinent than in an exploration of the function of fictional worlds in general. The ending foregrounds effectively what has served as a background for the various strands of the plot, the function of Art. If works of art are necessarily fictions, then what is their value? In this respect, the final response of the I Ching serves as the "key to the treasure."[5] Juliana interprets the hexagram literally as a signal of the fictionality of the frightening world she lives in, but the hexagram may be interpreted more figuratively: all versions of reality are necessarily fictional, but that does not mean they are invalid;

they may reveal an inner truth, the truth that lies beneath surfaces, behind appearances. From this perspective the novel speaks to the larger issue of the function of fiction. Both novels—Abendsen's *Grasshopper Lies Heavy* and Dick's *Man in the High Castle*—are fictions, and the fraudulence of the text within the text contaminates the text that contains it: Dick's novel is as made-up as Abendsen's. But both fictions can lead characters to confront momentarily the question of their own "inner truth" or can reveal to an entire society the nature of its inner truth.

And so Dick's *Man in the High Castle,* despite its patent fraudulence, asserts its own relevance through its claim to inner truth. The logic that applies to *The Grasshopper Lies Heavy* by analogy applies to the novel that contains it. And the logic of Dick's novel suggests that the world in which we live—the America of the 1960s and 1970s—may not be that different from the one that Tagomi and Baynes and the Frinks must deal with. The novel tells us first that values, like individual perspectives on reality, are not absolute, that they are very much shaped by historical forces. The novel tells us in addition that, like the characters in the world of *The Man in the High Castle,* we live in a world in which "the madmen are in power"[6] because the people in power see themselves as agents, not victims, of history, because they believe they are godlike, and because they cannot realize or understand humanity's essential *helplessness.*[7] (This attitude has its roots in the whole notion of Western scientism and empiricism that conceives the natural world as something "out there" to be known and subjugated, an epistemological assumption that Dick questions.) One critic summarizes some of the implications of this motif of the novel as follows: "The mirror of fiction reveals an image of truth; the artist is the one who knows the answer. Hawthorne Abendsen is right, but so is *his* creator. Nazi violence, the historical equivalent of the spiritual futility and chaos of modern America, rules the world, and the Nuremberg trial—an act of Justice—is only a dream."[8]

Dick's most important message, aside from his analysis of fictionality, concerns the relativity of questions of good and evil. Dick's narrative method and his narrative *donnée* seem to suggest that relativism permeates the fabric of our lives—the way we experience the world and the values we adopt. But Dick's novel suggests, at least through the auspices of the sympathetically rendered character Tagomi, that this relativism does not obtain to the question of the existence of evil. Tagomi comes to this realization at an early point in the text ("There is evil! It's actual like cement. I can't believe it. I can't stand it. Evil is not a view.'')[9] and nothing in the text tends to controvert his epiphany. This motif in the novel comes to a conclusion in Baynes' meditations upon his return to Germany to fight Operation Dandelion:

> The terrible dilemma of our lives. Whatever happens, it is evil beyond compare. Why struggle, then? Why choose? If all alternatives are the same . . .
> Evidently we go on, as we always have. From day to day. At this moment we work against Operation Dandelion. Later on, at another moment, we work to defeat the police. But we cannot do it all at once; it is a sequence. An unfolding process. We can only control the end by making a choice at each step.
> He thought, We can only hope. And try.
> On some other world, possibly it is different. Better. There are clear good and evil alternatives. Not these obscure admixtures, these blends, with no proper tool by which to untangle the components.
> We do not have the ideal world, such as we would like, where morality is easy because cognition is easy. Where one can do right with no effort because he can detect the obvious.[10]

One thing that enables us to deal with the "terrible dilemma of our lives," something that Tagomi naturally turns to in his time of need by trying to wrest solace from Frink's jewelry,[11] (is) works of art, whether in plastic, graphic, or verbal form. The novel's plot unfolds for readers the stories of various "lower-place" Americans who are exposed to Art in one form or another and whose lives are changed for the better as a consequence: egged on by a fellow craftsman, Frank Frink gives up his lackey position making copies of authentic Americana, begins to design original jewelry, and in so doing achieves both independence and personal integrity; Robert Childan, when circumstances thrust Frink's jewelry into his life, refuses to "sell out" to Japanese entrepreneurs and instead becomes middleman for a new line of original American art; and Juliana, having discovered the truth of Abendsen's novel, draws from the revelation a measure of freedom, of peace, in a life until then characterized by turmoil and restlessness.

As metafictional Art, Dick's novel reveals its own fraudulence, as if to emphasize its illusionary nature at the same time it insists upon its ultimate significance. For Dick's point is that even if art creates illusory worlds, there is a purpose to illusion: "Odd, he thought. Vital sometimes to be merely cardboard front, like carton. Bit of satori there, if I could lay hold of it. Purpose in overall scheme of illusion, could we but fathom. Law of economy: nothing is waste. Even the unreal. What a sublimity in the process."[12] The illusionary, the unreal, is not merely decorative or simply entertaining. Beneath the surface or behind the appearance, actuality goes on "could we but fathom." And Baynes' analysis indicates that science fiction is particularly well suited to reveal actualities and alternatives by presenting readers with other worlds in which distinctions are clearer because cognition is easy. Science fiction gives readers alternate worlds that foster cognition and, so Dick would argue, thus encourage us to go on.

In this emphasis upon the possibilities inherent in the imagining of other worlds, Dick singles out the quality that marks science fiction as a narrative subgenre and that provides it with its particular promise. We can use Dick's insight as a place of departure for an examination of the generic distinctiveness of science fiction, an enterprise that necessarily begins with an analysis of fiction and fictional worlds in general. All fiction, in that it is necessarily mediated (someone stands between the reader and the narrated events), presents its audience with two main systems of signification, what we might term the "space" of the speaker and the "space" of the fictional world. Various modes of fiction can be distinguished and characterized according to discriminations made in terms of type of speaker or in terms of the nature of the fictional world. For example, some critics attempt to discriminate among fictions according to the person, number, and stance of the mediating subject; these critics classify fictions according to their "point of view."[13] Yet another way to distinguish among fictional forms is to specify the nature of the fictional world. This tool has been a standard of critics ever since Clara Reeve in *The Progress of Romance* (1785) used it to distinguish between Novel and Romance.[14] Any study that purports to establish generic distinctions between fictional forms necessarily relies on comparisons between the fictional world and the "real world," since the relation of Fiction and Reality is at the root of genre theory.

It follows axiomatically that the subgenre of science fiction can best be described by studying the nature of its fictional world, a truth that many readers of science fiction come to inductively or intuitively. Science fiction can be identified by its peculiarly "science-fictional" world. The essential question then becomes, How can we describe the worlds of science fiction?

The first step obviously is to describe the components of fictional worlds in general. Working inductively, from a basic understanding of the constituents of a world, one can posit two major components of any fictional world, roughly equivalent to the lexicon and syntax of a language—its "World" and its "Story." By the former we intend the total stock of possible fictional entities—that is, the people, places, and objects that "occupy" the imaginal space of the fiction. When discussing a World, to avoid implicit assumptions that the characters are human and the settings terran and therefore predictable and familiar, I shall use the terms "actants" and 'topoi"; a World consists of a number of actants who populate, occupy, or exist in any number of specified or implicit topoi. By the Story of a fictional world, I mean the concatenation of events and actions that take place within the space of the world, regardless of their magnitude, plausibility, or interconnectedness. At the abstract level Story combines the various entities that make up the World; it consists of the systematic set of rules governing the order and arrangement of actants and motifs.

The second step in our definition involves establishing a standard with which to compare the object of inquiry. In this respect Lubomir Dolezel offers the following suggestion: "The study of possible narrative worlds will be facilitated, if we can define a *basic* narrative world to which all other possible narrative worlds will be related as its alternatives. It seems natural to propose for this role the narrative world which corresponds to our actual, empirical world."[15] The concept of "basic narrative world" entails necessarily a relationship of correspondence that dictates that statements made about that world cannot contradict statements that might be made about our own "real world."

Armed with these postulates, we can begin to make some discriminations about the nature of science-fictional worlds. We can specify, to begin with, that what particularly distinguishes the fictional world of science fiction is not its Story but its World, which stands in a peculiar but definable relation with the basic narrative world. The various Stories of science fiction, once divested of their otherworldly appurtenances, tend to coincide with the Stories available to fiction set in the basic narrative world.[16] For this reason, one cannot use the component of Story as the basis for a discrimination of the genre of science fiction, as some critics (or anthologies) tend to do when they identify standard science-fictional motifs, that is, encounter with an alien, adventures in space, the postholocaust world. These motifs are available in modified form to realistic or naturalistic fiction. Having elminated Story, we must focus on the World of science fiction, in particular, on the transformations it works on the basic narrative world.

Samuel Delany, in a very interesting article entitled "About 5,175 Words," notes that all fiction exists at a certain level of subjunctivity. Naturalistic fiction, which accepts as its domain the basic narrative world, exists at a level of subjunctivity defined by the phrase, *could have happened* (implicit in our definition of basic narrative world). Other forms of fiction exist at other levels of subjunctivity; the "mood" for fantasy fiction, for example, is *could not have happened*. Delany identifies the level of subjunctivity for science fiction as *has not happened* and goes on to enumerate the possibilities that inhere in this particular narrative ontology.[17] His general point is well taken. *The* distinctive feature of science fiction rests in its generic license to create worlds that are other than the world we know. This license identifies science fiction as a narrative species belonging to what is traditionally known as romance (and remember that Wells referred to his fictions as "scientific romances"). When we pick up a text that purports to be science fiction, we automatically make certain assumptions about that text, among them that it will not re-present (represent) reality, that it will rather add itself to the world. It is as if there were written in bold letters across the cover of the text the words *as if*, signalling the peculiar essence of the fictional world. Several writers have pointed to this quality of science fiction: Le Guin, in a preface to *The Left Hand of Darkness,* refers to the disjunction between science-fictional and basic narrative worlds as the product of a "thought experiment"; Darko Suvin in a seminal essay designates the otherness of the world as a source of "cognitive estrangement"; and Robert Scholes argues that science fiction creates its worlds by means of a "representational discontinuity."[18] For our purposes Scholes' formulation is the most useful in that it specifies that the fundamental discontinuity is representational, which suggests that the essential transformation involves what we have termed "World."

Before we speak of the types of transformations, it is necessary to mention some of the advantages that accrue to this kind of narrative ontology. The obvious advantage is the amount of creative freedom granted the author. The author who sets out to write science fiction is relieved of some of the pressures of "reality"; he or she is free to speculate, to fabulate, to invent. But the conventions of science fiction do not grant total license to the fictionist. Once the author has posited the "representational discontinuity," the conventions of the genre dictate that the author thereafter adhere to the laws of nature and the "laws" inherent in the scientific method, for example, cause and effect, before and after, continuity of space and time. As one critic has noted, science fiction possesses a "deep structure that unites in some way scientific necessity and imaginative freedom."[19] This adherence to the dictates of scientific necessity distinguishes science fiction from fantasy in general. More importantly, it determines the range of functions that science fiction is able to serve.

As writers such as Aristotle, Horace, and Henry Fielding have noted, the primary functions of art of any kind are to entertain and to instruct. The unique narrative ontology of science fiction particularly enables it to fulfill these functions. The simple fact of otherness of the fictional world insures to some degree that the fiction will entertain; there is a certain fascination—whether antipathetic, xenophobic, intellectual, or sympathetic—generated by that which is unfamiliar or strange. As a matter of fact, the Russian Formalists tended to single out the act of "defamiliarization" as the *sine qua non* of the Literary.[20] In any case, the strangeness of science-fictional worlds guarantees that they will satisfy some sublimative needs.

But, as Scholes and others have pointed out, it is not enough that fiction answer our unspoken fears and desires; we also insist that it from time to time help us to know ourselves or teach us something about the way we live now. A fiction that takes as its domain the basic narrative world almost automatically "announces" that the lessons learned by its actants within the "space" of the fiction obtain in the world outside the text. The epiphanies of the characters are valid insights into the "nature of reality" both within and without the text. Jonathan Culler has argued that "making sense" of fictional texts consists in discovering and applying the correct culturally sanctioned models of *vraisemblance* (an untranslatable world connoting the systematic nature of correspondence between literary texts and the text of the real). The first two such models he discusses derive directly from experiential reality; they involve an awareness either of what is "real" or of what is general human knowledge.[21]

Clearly these models of *vraisemblance* are not available to the reader of science fiction who is confronted by a world that proclaims its difference from the "real." The reader must discover or invent other models in order to recuperate or "naturalize" a science-fictional world. Now the fact that the text adheres to the logic of scientific method and natural law in part assures the reader that retrieval is possible, that relations of correspondence do exist. The World of the fiction is regular and predictable within limits, and standards of comparison can therefore be established. And part of the attraction of science fiction texts rests in the fact that the systems of correspondence between real and fictional worlds are generated primarily by the labor of the reader. The reader knows that he or she must work to achieve cognitive satisfactions. The challenge of all serious science fiction lies in the working out of its *vraisemblance*.

Despite the fact that various science fictions may be recuperated variously, we may tentatively identify the kinds of transformations that science fiction works upon components of World and the forms of recuperation these transformations entail. We have argued that a World comprises in a set of actants who exist continuously in any number of topoi. We should add that the configurations of those topoi (not to mention the morphology of the actants) presuppose a system of natural laws. We can say then that the components of any world are three: actants, topoi, implicit system of natural laws. Now a science-fictional world may be created by transforming or introducing an alien element into any one of these components. The contamination of the basic narrative world by something other introduces a factor of discontinuity between "reality" and fiction. The fiction swerves from fantasy in general toward science fiction if, after the factor of discontinuity is introduced (and the factor might involve both actants and topoi), the fiction adheres to a logic that accords with scientific method and natural law. For example, the appearance of talking animals must be scientifically *motivated,* in the sense of accounted for (as is not the case in fairy tales).[22]

It might be helpful to discuss the transformation of each component of World in turn. The transformation of the system of actants involves the introduction of alien entities into a system that is totally human in "realistic" fiction. One or more of the actants are entities that are nonhuman or superhuman or subhuman. The Story paradigm for a fiction using this transformation might be "encounter with an alien," and a representative example might be Clarke's *Childhood's End.* The reader recuperates this type of fiction by comparing human and alien entities. The fiction tends to broach the question, "What is it to be human?"; the cognitive thrust involves better understanding of self and other. Transformations of topoi occur in fictions that locate the skeleton of Story in spatial dimensions, geographical domains, or cultural milieus that are essentially other; some factor of the topos makes it physically other, or logically impossible, removed in space or time. The Story paradigm for this fiction might be the visit to a utopic or dystopic society, and a representative example might be Heinlein's *Moon Is a Harsh Mistress*. The cognitive thrust of this type deals with knowledge of self and society. Readers are encouraged to investigate their nature as social animals by comparing the fictional society with their own. Fictions incorporating one or more transformations of natural law (for example, the introduction of magic) might be referred to as "science fantasy," and, like fantasy in general, often serve ends other than cognitive. Science fantasy frequently asks of its readers that they gape in awe at its wonder-filled world, or that they delight in the purely intellectual complications or conundrums that the suspension of natural law gives rise to. Story paradigms for this transformation might be the *voyage extraordinaire* or the time-travel story, and a representative example might be Verne's *Voyage to the Center of the Earth*.

It should be obvious that we have not nearly exhausted the possibilities of analysis here. For example, one could distinguish not only among the components of World but between types of discontinuity. Some critics of science fiction have suggested that the degree of discontinuity is dependent upon the kind of mental operation involved—the discontinuity can be produced by "extrapolation" or by "speculation."[23] This kind of distinction might be overlaid on the notion of transformation to multiply possible discriminations and thus refine the critical apparatus. And the whole notion of models of *vraisemblance* for science-fictional worlds needs to be explored and elaborated. What is clear to me at this point is that the generic distinctiveness of science fiction is generated by the nature of its fictional world, that the genre can be described with reference to that world, and that the cognitive value of the genre, value that is more and more taken for granted, lies in this discrepancy between science-fictional world and basic narrative world. And, of course, it is just this value that writers such as Philip Dick are aware of, just this value that ultimately justifies the enterprise of science fictionists in general, for "on some other world, possibly it is different. Better. There are clear good and evil alternatives. Not these obscure admixtures, these blends, with no proper tool by which to untangle the components." Science fiction can be the proper tool.

The Past of Science Fiction

Thomas A. Hanzo

No special effects were needed to film the first version of *The Invasion of the Body Snatchers,* produced on a low budget with a high potential for critical analysis. In that story the only contrivance is the happy ending. What is there anticipated for the human race has a certain authority: human beings are duplicated in podlike growths, and, like peas in those pods, they are psychologically the same, possessing no individuating consciousness and deriving their strength from a shared unity of mind and purpose. The story capitalizes on the sinister aspects of such a gain in power, but it is one of the most popular themes in the genre, and it is fitting, at least for the way in which the theme will be considered here, that it be associated with that birth in the egglike pod. The origin is similar in many tales of monsters, from the kind that destroy Tokyo after their eggs have been released by an atomic blast to the silicon atoms of *The Andromeda Strain* that multiply with such deadly rapidity. In all such tales, the birth is of a spark of life that is revived after aeons of sleep; it is a restored life, a return from some prehistoric and prehuman past of such antiquity—or such distance—that its nature is wholly alien and, most frequently, utterly hostile to humanity. If it could, it would draw us all down to that archaic time, and from our own mythological past, the same kind of danger threatens. The monster Typhon, who cannot be slain but only suppressed, belongs to an age earlier than that of the hero who confronts him; his power derives from the Great Mother, who antedates the Olympian Zeus. The fact that, even in the most debased popular forms of the story, the creature from the past cannot be destroyed, suggests its psychological sources. In the past there is something deathless, which does not

131

know death and which therefore, by the irrefutable logic of the psyche, also does not know what it is to possess and to be an individual consciousness. The conjunction of the themes prepares us for a shock of recognition: the genre of the future returns us, paradoxically, to a past.

The ubiquity of the return I shall return to later. That the future belongs to our genre, not as its virtual fate (of the future of the genre as genre we would all, I think, be wise to be silent), but as an indispensable and given element of its structure of ideas, is at least assumed in every definition I know of. Kingsley Amis says that the genre treats "of a situation that could not arise in the world we know, but which is hypothesized on the basis of some innovation in science or technology. . . ."[1] "Hypothesized" reminds us of all those theories of extrapolation and prediction that have bedeviled and, in some extreme instances, disgraced this branch of fiction. But whether, with certain hard-liners, we see the future in science fiction only as a kind of rational extrapolation from the present state of scientific knowledge or whether it is less rigorously projected as a future of psychological or social things to come, the genre asserts that that open dimension is its characteristic ground. Space may be its scene, the extraterrestrial its locale, but time is its peculiar realm; the future gives science fiction its energy and purpose.

There is a term for this fictional structure. In rhetoric, when the future is treated as the past, a prolepsis has been employed: what is to come, as a tactic of persuasion, is put into the past tense. In order to fix its events in a future, the narrative of science fiction also creates a future that is past, a time that is moving through a future, making a past of that future. Science fiction is a proleptic structure, unfolding a future that as the narrative proceeds becomes a past. The device is flexible enough to accommodate extremes: Larry Niven and Jerry Pournelle in *Lucifer's Hammer* may take up their story in what we assume is the present, but, in the immediacies of this narrative, the discovery of the comet occurs in a future that forms the past out of which the events of the narrative, all now safely in the future of science fiction, will develop. Prolepsis may be too formidable a term to some or to others merely reductive and simplistic, but that it designates a universal feature of the genre and a common assumption of its critics seems reason enough to allow it to serve here for its analytic usefulness.

I began by suggesting that, paradoxically, given its stake in the future, science fiction can be said to excavate a past and that, as a matter of narrative progression, it must convert that future into a past. From another point of view, to know a future is to know a past. I am going to attempt to say that the Second and Third foundations, and fourth and fifth no doubt, the "billion-year spree" itself, belong to our past. I want to approach the question of the past that is the future of science fiction in part thematically and then, more importantly for us, structurally, for despite the fact that it projects a future, science fiction is compelled by its very limits, by its formal necessities, by its status as a mode, as a genre, of fiction, to return us to the past. Its proleptic form is complicated and intensified by the fact that science fiction brings us back to our personal and ultimately to our unconscious past. If all narratives convert their projected futures into a past, science fiction earns its characteristic proleptic form by insisting that that narrative past remain in the future, and there in the future these imaginative anticipations produce substitutes for what has been lost. They restore a past. And even in the substance of these dreams, the past is recovered, for, as it makes the future a past, the narrative draws upon a past already lived, an historic past that will become finally the end that is the psychological beginning.

Historic time serves psychological need in this genre, as some well-known and complex novels will suggest. The themes in Frank Herbert's *Dune* proliferate with the abandon of the Fremen warriors in battle; what concerns us here is the idea of the desert culture itself, with its frequent recollections that under those marvelously contrived stillsuits beat the hearts of Bedouin tribes who have roamed the deserts of the Near East and Africa since time immemorial. Herbert imports his science from faintly illegal laboratories on distant planets, the technological moonshiners of the Imperium, but for *Dune* he preserves the heritage of that religious-military fanaticism that Paul Muad'dib is said to fear. This past is the consciously apprehended historic past that belongs to us all as the present inhabitants of Earth, and to it science fiction writers persistently return with undiminished interest. It is the past of the postatomic ages of Miller's *Canticle for Leibowitz,* the Medieval-Renaissance-Atomic Cycle that, in some future, repeats our own history. To it Joanna Russ returns in *Picnic on Paradise,* when her travelers on their incomprehensible mission encounter trials like those of a hundred explorers of our remote and even recent history. Ursula Le Guin similarly in *Left Hand of Darkness* sends Genly Ai and Estraven on a journey across snow that recalls our polar explorers, and, in many a science fiction adventure, the historic past is recovered and preserved again and again: ancient man appears, as do the tribes of the steppes, the populations of the great ancient cities, and, to come to more recent historic times, Hitler and youth gangs and a hundred variations on the manners and morals of the race. Without exaggeration it can be said that much science fiction drifts as though in a kind of archaic field of temporal magnetism toward what we might call a hyperpast, a veritable black hole of pastness, of prehistory and geologic time, the time of the antehuman. The number of novels that explore this realm would, I think, astonish us if we were to count them. There are the tribal societies of Piers Anthony's *Battle Circle* trilogy; there are Anne McCaffrey's *Dinosaur Planet*, Philip José Farmer's *Time's Last Gift* and, to mention a novel I shall return to later, Brian Aldiss's *Cryptozoic*, with its remarkable version of that proleptic structure under discussion here.

The past of the future of science fiction is compounded and confused by another of its forms, by an unconscious time, a time past that belongs to no history and that is prior to the emergence of historic man or man as an individual human being. This past—psychological, spiritual, or mythical—when intensified as a distant future is more likely to recur as the lost past. As in all such time, its determining feature is its infinite remoteness; it is the time of birth, of beginning, or rebirth, as well as of the end, the time when the present world gives way to the new that recapitulates the old. In *Dune* this unconscious, atemporal, psychological past is represented by the Bene Gesserit training, when Reverend Mothers live as the embodiment, dangerous though it may be, of the entire line of those Mothers who have in their care, they hope, the emergence or birth of a Savior. In Paul Atreides, however, and later in his son, the facility is immensely increased so that it is united with an equally dangerous prescience; the genetic union with the past implies by a kind of mental law that the future is implicit in what happened, that unity itself must extend to infinity. Then, when Leto Atreides assumes leadership, unity is enlarged again, and his nearly deathless reign is accomplished both by the life he shares with his progenitors and by his assumption of a community of identity with another life form. In this feature of the past of science fiction, man lives in what appears to be the ideal unity with the other, the dream of many writers, which psychologically recovers that original unit that, in the life of every individual, is remembered unconsciously as the identity with the mother. Child psychologists have described this time of unity and separation in many ways, though I prefer to adopt the Freudian view that the event persists as the memory of a loss and that, to some extent, all desire has as its motive the replacement, to some degree, of this original unity. The future becomes the past, then; the desired, ultimate unity replicates the lost unity of unconscious childhood. In *Canticle for Leibowitz,* the child who grows on the old woman is the innocent one of our past. Clarke's *Childhood's End* molds this element of the past of the future of science fiction in its own way, but the essential element of the unconscious past of our prehistory remains: the children, united in a hyperconsciousness that is nothing else again than our own lost unconscious unity, abandon earthly temporalities altogether.

It is a super- and supraconsciousness that, because it is by definition not available to normal consciousness and therefore most precisely not to the narrative consciousness of the text, differentiates itself from consciousness as an unconsciousness. That phase of our psychic life, we know, adheres rigidly to our past. The problem of representing these altered states of consciousness, as a kind of quasi-scientific interest calls them (an interest that should not be thought of as more than pseudoscience), is that language, which belongs to consciousness, cannot reach these super- or unconscious experiences. Efforts to represent them in narrative generally have failed; though Herbert himself has been assiduously practicing the art, the passages throughout the *Dune* trilogy that make the attempt are the least successful, the most tiring of the novels. These representations of what lies outside of or beyond consciousness (the spatial metaphors are nearly unavoidable) ought to be distinguished from narrative presentations of aspects of experience that lie below the threshold of fully conscious thought, in the prereflective and sensuous consciousness. Samuel Delany in *Triton,* for example, writes, "lights here and there, in his streaming eyes, lit fragments of an unreal city."[2] The experience could be attributed to Benjy of *The Sound and the Fury* or to Bloom of *Ulysses;* if not wholly direct, it is also not reflected experience, or experience reflected upon. But this general narrative problem, both in its technical and thematic implications, differs from what I am suggesting here, that the futurism of science fiction conveys us, and is expressed as, a return to a past, as narrative, as history, and as psychological state.

The past of the future may be simple or complex, but the logic of this futural structure, particularly in its psychological dimension, holds with remarkable consistency under many guises and in various manifestations. According to this logic, if the representations we have so briefly examined are to be trusted, the future, as a constituting element of a sociocultural linguistic structure, first draws the narrative through a projected time, sometimes a quite immediate future, sometimes (the last acts of Blish's Flying Cities are examples) the very distant future that is the cosmic beginning, and sometimes that mysterious conjunction where space-time is given another perspective, as in Stapledon's visions or in Fred Saberhagen's *Berserker Man*. The future so imagined acquires, by virtue of the narrative act itself, a past, but this narrative temporality serves another past, a past that presents one or both of two aspects: the past of our consciously appropriated history as a cultural datum and the past in which was experienced a loss that the future may restore. These are two very different pasts, though they may be mixed in various degrees, but by definition they are mutually annihilating, for to discover the end of time is to destroy history, and to be abandoned to history is to suffer the primeval loss forever. When the reader comes to the text of science fiction, the expectation that its time is a future will always be granted, but it is a relatively empty and banal expectation that must be supported by another that establishes the reader in his less conscious anticipation of a relation to his present world. As Jonathan Culler puts it, a genre is a "particular relation to the world which serves as norm or expectation to guide the reader in his encounter with the text."[3] The relation in science fiction is to a world conceived as future and made concrete as a past.

To describe a literary structure, if we are to take the structuralist method seriously, requires us not only to alter the methodology we design to cope with the interpretation of literature, but also to revise our conception of literariness and of textuality. The project is to characterize genre by discovering the conditions of meaning it imposes; not to interpret, but to define the possibilities of interpretation; not to gather all the meanings, the full meaning, but to describe, so to speak, the empty meaning. For science fiction, if we omit now the effects of narrative technique itself, two versions of the past of its future establish such conditions and possibilities of meaning, that is, the historical past and the buried past of the unconscious. Vulgar as well as sophisticated works are instructive in this regard: *Close Encounters of the Third Kind* returns Richard Dreyfus to a particularly delightful if nebulously childlike universe where the unity of musical harmony prevails; in *Star Wars* medieval swordsmen and knights in black and white armor clash with satisfying displays of strength and firearms; and *Star Wars,* too, bows to the inevitable return to an unconscious suprapersonal unity whenever the Force is invoked.

Ursula Le Guin, who understands the genre perhaps as well as anyone, plays in masterful fashion with these possibilities in *The*

Lathe of Heaven. George Orr dreams reality, and there begins his responsibility, for the reality so produced requires that the past be altered to account for it. Here the narrative past varies its presentation of a historical past, and after the power falls into the hands of the mad psychiatrist, Le Guin arouses the other condition of meaning by introducing, through George's dreams, the Aliens, who perfectly understand his abilities and the reason for his failures to control that power. According to these nonhumans, the power is a suprapersonal one, reserved rightly for those species who do not possess the individual, and limiting, human consciousness. All time-travel narratives, particularly those that posit the power to alter the past, emphasize in both directions of the travel that the historic past is being revisited. Wells' hero, who in *The Time Machine* strikes the predictive note, finds a remote future time that takes us back to a tragic version of the beginning: man, who possesses reason and feeling that war with each other, finally suffers a dissolution into his component elements. Ultimately the Earth itself returns to its lifeless origins. The farther into the future we imagine ourselves, so might a principle governing science fiction be stated, the more likely we are to be placed at the beginning of time and so at the origin of things, or, by following some obscure psychological necessity, at the time of prepersonal, unconscious unity. History, advanced far enough, achieves its end in its beginnings, as the cosmic model of the pulsing universe suggests. On the physical level, where entropy reigns, all excitation eventually is dissipated, and the original state is resumed. In the psyche of man, the equivalent movement is into and beyond consciousness, or, since it is only consciousness that we know, out of the darkness and back into darkness, regardless of what wonders of existence we impute to that as yet to be achieved state on the other side of consciousness.

Literary conventions assemble themselves with a certain logic, as in Frye's cycle of modes, and the identification of these aggregates is possible because of their relations to each other. What genres adjoin or abut science fiction? It is a question Frye's system might answer quickly, perhaps too glibly for some, in ruminations about romance, but for our purposes I should like to suggest three areas of difference-resemblance to other genres. In the first, a resemblance of a low order of interest separates science fiction from historical fiction; the past in the historical novel is not a function of futurity, but rather another time, in custom, habits, and institutions, valued for its simple difference from our own (quaintness, antiquarian interest) or for its valued distinction (it engendered our time; it illustrates what is true of our time). In either case it is discovered as what has been and cannot be again. Historical fiction selects a past as known—what happened—and converts this epoch into the environment of the action and into the condition of the present. In science fiction the past, however well known as the past of a human history, is retold in relation to that projected future that is the essential dimension of the fiction.

As the material of the future, the past is rediscovered, repeated in a new key, and given a new emotional valuation. When we sit with Brother Francis Gerard outside Leibowitz Abbey, we are ready to assume the rules of the monastic order, but, having already lived them as part of the social and intellectual history of the West, we are also prepared to assume a critical, historical awareness of their development and decline. To relive historical reality in a future is to feel its evanescence, to recognize the fragility of the temporal structure of human institutions and society, to become aware of one's own mortality, and to live, in short, in a projection of one's own death that is canceled not by its futurity (it will happen, but not now) but by futurity itself. There is a future where the past will exist again, where—so we may paraphrase this mood—the death of the past will be understood, and where it lies to be experienced again. Since we cannot experience our own death, we live in projections of it that deny it, and science fiction obeys this contradiction. Historical fiction discovers its own way of denying what it affirms of death, but in science fiction futurity itself promises and then withholds the end. What is not so apparent in this dynamics of temporality is that the historic past is so visible, so much the stuff of the genre. Another relation of the genre to its neighbors seems useful to explore now, that of science fiction to fantasy.

In distinction to the fiction that extrapolates, that, in a wide sense, projects the possible into a future, fantasy breaks just that connection with the possible and emphasizes the alterity rather than the futurity of the fictionalized environment. Naturally, linkages abound: *The Left Hand of Darkness* is otherworldly, in more than the planetary sense, but its science is a technology conventionally linked to our own; *Voyage to Arcturus,* on the other hand, is in the place of otherness and produces the disexpected and astonishment, in Eric Rabkin's terms,[4] with an unforgettable inventiveness. Such comparisons are instructive; yet to assume, as does Todorov, that each genre aspires to a logical exhaustion of its distinguishing feature—such as the use of the supernatural—seems to me a false assumption about literary genre as well as a misapprehension of structuralist principles.[5] This is no occasion to argue these points, but that otherness of fantasy, the displacement of worldhood to what is magical, to what defies expectation, to what is opposed to reality appears to avoid contact altogether with science fiction. In science fiction the expected, the essentially rational connection with the future, tends to be asserted. To engender a future by assessing the present would seem a rejection of the premises underlying fantasy; to move into another time differs profoundly, if this distinction of genres holds, from being transported into a different place. The difference is not absolute, however, as the more imaginative speculative fiction of Le Guin and others suggests. Magic, strangeness, irreality, lack of the rules of expectation—all these elements have invaded or crossed the barrier between the two genres freely and without apparent discomfort to most readers. In relation to the unconscious past of science fiction, another possible common frontier between the two modes of imaginative projection will be suggested later, but by way of turning now to another literary type that antedates our categories.

Northrop Frye has convincingly drawn upon certain literary forms he finds best exemplified in religious scriptures as the most comprehensive representatives of the literary universe he so much invokes and beguilingly imagines. For a growing body of readers, science fiction has gradually come to satisfy whatever profound expectations and needs used to be fulfilled in scripture. Works such as the *Foundation* series and *Stranger in a Strange Land* and many others sound the apocalyptic note of the world's scriptures, or, to adopt Frye's set of contraries, either the apocalyptic or demonic imagery proper to the form. These works anticipate not merely the future but the end of the future, not only a development and a possibility but the final cause as well, the teleological structure of the world. In cosmic anticipation they invoke the ultimate future as they gaze back upon the past to organize or dispose of it, perhaps to plant new life or, in the face of universal mystery, to wonder that it occurred, when it may never occur again. I have suggested that in one use of the past the future's destiny commonly takes the form of an idea of suprapersonal, unconscious, universal unity, even if only, for some cataclysmic-minded writers, in the final fury of an implosion that reduces all existence to the same dense material. But that aspiration, that buried wish for an extinction in nonpersonal unity, is also a wish to return; in its mythological extension it is a movement toward rebirth. Even this exploding universe apparently dances toward that climactic time when all shall be one again. Stapledon's epic perhaps best illustrates this view, though in a lesser story told with equal portentousness—the hallucinogenic light show *2001*—the conclusion is reached when the hero returns transformed into a child encased in an egg gazing from its transcendent point of view at humankind, its consciousness altered, converted to a supernal, childlike innocence. The race gives birth to a new and universal consciousness that transcends space and time. This apocalyptic vision is science fiction as scripture, the future united with the past, when the future produces the egg from which the past itself emerged and from which the past may now be contemplated. What was lost is regained, to be possessed anew. The end is the beginning. The conclusion of the billion-year spree is that ultimate orgasm in which, at the same moment, we both destroy and create ourselves. The apocalyptic and demonic are united, as at the bottom of Dante's Inferno, in these all-embracing metaphors for the infinity as well as for the limits of human desire.[6]

The structure of the genre imposes this organizing impulse and these conditions of meaning: the past, the historical past that belongs to humanity, becomes the material for a redirection and a revision in a future that turns back upon itself toward some nonpersonal existence; an intense consciousness of history, perhaps merely the sign of our rationalized historical consciousness, is compensated for and transformed by the return to oblivion. These conditions and modulations of meanings do not convert science fiction into myth; they are, in Paul Ricoeur's sense, reflections upon myth,[7] the self-conscious reflections upon myth, from the point of view of one living in history, that may become philosophy, but that in the genre of science fiction articulate its thematic-structural possibilities. These generic ways of relating to the human world, perhaps like all such fundamental attitudes, reconcile opposites and allow us to live in ambiguity. To find the origin in the future, to realize a lost unity in a psychological development yet to come, to recover the dream of a greater consciousness in the dark perception of a new and undifferentiated consciousness, to reflect from an ahistorical point of view upon historicity itself—these are the intentions that determine, it seems to me, the modes and patterns of the genre. Of course science fiction cannot do without the human past; where else, we should ask, will it discover its materials? Of course it cannot escape the boundaries of a human psyche that desires, hopes, and dreams according to patterns that are organized in the earliest movements of instinctual need. What is more interesting and more to our purpose here is to reflect upon the quality and the cultural significance of these imaginative purposes. Why this reckless thrusting of ourselves upon the dim future? Why the popularity of such themes as technological salvation or damnation, alien invasion, alien superiority, ultimate annihilation, radical otherness, permanent dispossession, and the like?

It cannot be my ambition here to reply authoritatively to these questions. Perhaps, as Frank Kermode suggests,[8] we require grand organizing fictions to draw our world into a humanized, intelligible whole, and science fiction, in an age of discordance, has become one of our concord fictions, sometimes by intention and always through this genre's manner of relating to the world through actualizations of a future. Perhaps science fiction is another of a series of attempts to confront and master the terror of time—time the limitless, time the devourer, time the agent of pure seriality against which all our need for order and all our desire to recapture a lost past are minor local disturbances in the vast fabric of space-time. Perhaps, as Kermode suggests, we suffer in our own way from the same kind of anxiety— the eschatological anxiety—that troubled Mesopotamian culture as well as the late sixteenth century. Crisis awareness and its accompanying shudders of cataclysmic anticipation perhaps belong to our century as to no other, except, if Barbara Tuchman is correct, to the plague years of the fourteenth. But of the limitless we can know nothing, as the great scriptures and science fiction both declare; our business is with our own lives and with the values we find in them.

Oceanic feelings of despair and futility may sometimes overwhelm the worlds of science fiction, but resolutions and assumptions are as frequently hopeful and aspiring. Curiously, in the genre that posited the future as the triumph of the technical, it is frequently just the opposite that has sustained its hope. In his fascinating *Berserker,* where Fred Saberhagen imagines with chilling persuasiveness the utter hostility of the perfectly unhuman machine, development is associated not with a new order of mechanical, technological perfection but with man himself. Like Herbert's hero Leto, Michel Geulinex somehow achieves a new consciousness in a symbiotic relationship, though on this occasion with a kind of sentient machine. When extrapolated infinitely, technology, usually, is wholly alien, the demonic creation that technology even in its infancy promised. For the genre as I have approached it, the future may be said to be created out of a past in a linear monopoly of meaning—pure technology—to create an antihuman destiny, while what is given to man as a future—one that belongs to man as man—preserves his humanity, his values, and projects his own identity by discovering it within an enlarged community, though one that is realized at some more intense level of life or thought, usually, that is, through a more intensely shared life. In *Canticle for Leibowitz* the innocence of the child born without sin who inherits the Earth belongs to a new order of being. Fallen man, condemned to a cyclic pattern of history on Earth, rises toward the stars in the new community of space flight. The thrust toward the future, the risk of futurity, is taken as the hope that such new forms of community, new modes of love, new systems of communication, new domains of consciousness may be achieved; in all these, one feature is constant: the new consciousness is a common consciousness. The new life is a recovery of what—at least in this representation of the genre's possibilities—has been lost.

Of course, the new communities have failed too. The billion-year adventure contains many instances of interstellar migration that have lost their communal identities and ideas. Yet the new unity appears again and again with the unmistakable lineaments of being also the returned, or the origin that is the model of the unity that is essentially what must be recaptured. John Brunner's *Shockwave Rider* defies an electronic mockery of human communication by allowing the formation of a village society where to communicate is also to socialize. In dozens of similar fictional developments, the future returns quietly to some scene whose simplicity, grace, and human oneness identify it as that garden from which we all descend, that preconscious unity that is so often remembered in our fictions as the transpersonal identity of men yet to come.

The past that is conscious, the historic past of culture, itself finally serves in our fictions these forms of transcendent superconsciousness. I have accounted here for its desirability by drawing upon a kind of mythic tale, developed chiefly by child psychologists and psychoanalysts, of the emergence of an individuating consciousness out of an infant state of dependency and emotional oneness with the mother. In the apartness that accompanies consciousness, an anxiety grows, and a fantasy is engendered; the anxiety frequently is expressed as self-accusation (noticeably prominent in responses to loss such as grieving melancholy) and a fantasy that provides the pattern for all subsequent replacements of the original loss. The tendency is toward absorption in the beloved object, toward a kind of total identification with the object, whether that object is the self or the other. Through these psychic mechanisms, pervasive even in mature desire when narcissism and coalescence with the other are to some degree mastered, the ego seeks that relief that in effect means its own extinction. The signs of this recovery—this life through death—are as varied as the narrative imagination in science fiction can make them. The signs I have marked out range from the achievement of a superconsciousness to much less dramatic, but no less effective, supercommunities. The compensatory value of such achievements is to be balanced against the two discomforts, the two dangerous threats to a concordant existence, that science fiction continues to represent: on the one hand, the prison of history, endless repetition in time of a past that has produced the loss of human community; and on the other hand, in the same temporal dimension, though now linear rather than circular, the inhuman development of an ever more perfect technology. The projective energy of science fiction, its occupation with the future, is an effort to transcend or transform time, though by what must be seen now as contradictory and self-defeating means. Time, in the new consciousness or in the new community, is the realm, after all, of a past.

This mode of return, this repressed interest in recovering the past by means of projection into speculative futures, contrasts with the mode of fantasy and romance where it is the task of the adventurer to recover what is lost. In these genres, otherness is intensified to the point of human and even transhuman polarity. The Manichean world of romance and fantasy is populated by obstacles, pure otherness, in the form of human or bestial opposition, as well as by supernatural evils. These terrifying and alien othernesses, like demonic beings or sorcerers, always translate the self; they are nightmare agents, dream figures who enact aspects of the hero's self. Le Guin's *Earthsea* trilogy, with a truth we expect of her, particularly in the first volume, illustrates this point. The quest in romance is always for what has been displaced, for what once ruled, reigned, or could be loved, and is now gone. In the meantime, the other has risen in its place or bars the way to it. The Grail is the archetypal example, and the whole Arthurian cycle is complicated by the fact that in the quest another great value is being lost, that is, the community of the Round Table. Anne McCaffrey's Dragonriders sail out against the threads, but to find the origin and cause of that terrible curse. Perhaps now, if this representation of the intimate temporality of science fiction can be credited, its difference from fantasy may be clarified. The drive toward the future contains a suppressed return to a past. In fantasy the quest entails a restoration; it looks toward the past directly, in an experience of otherness, of opposition, of obstacles to be defeated, strangeness to be negotiated, the uncanny to be pacified. When we travel rather to the future, where temporal difference dominates, the new, the different, the alien are likely to present the past in another guise, not the known to be recovered, but the goal of time itself.

The reality we are reflecting upon here contains its own negation: time, or rather any emotional emphasis upon it such as we feel in science fiction, is likely to develop into one of those experiences of eternity that so often conclude the billion-year spree. The universe, spanned by faster-than-light travel, frequently inspires quasi-religious experiences of eternal oneness, and such travel itself is a denial that spurns and triumphs over time. One of its scriptural necessities is that science fiction shall look forward to this atemporality. Readers of science fiction who are lulled into believing such travel merely another technological marvel ignore the physical barriers to achieving such speeds and accept with remarkable calm what in fact are altered states of mind and not increases in velocity. Traveling faster than light would mean, as many science fiction writers know, leaving behind human existence itself. Time travel, too, displays this abandonment of the human; in a minor example of the genre by Barbara Paul, *Pillars of Salt,* the consequence of time travel, a dangerous one, is immortality. Alternate and parallel universes, on the other hand, defeat time in another way; Fredric Brown's *What Mad Universe* places the discovery of a space drive in our past. And the possibility of alternate or parallel worlds revives another aspect of the dream of infinity, for, as in Saberhagen's *Mask of the Sun,* the implication is that the existence of one other universe means the existence of an infinite number.

Omnipotence, infinity, allness, oneness, unity—these do not extend but limit the thematic possibilities of science fiction and, to return to the initial terms of our discussion, reveal its return to an ultimate psychological state, an origin that is a negation of time. To be out of time, indeed, is imagined as the end—both purpose and conclusion—of our being in time. As the phenomenologists have reminded us, temporality does not belong to us as a kind of attribute such as the color of our skins, but is constitutive of our beings; we are temporalized beings, living in a time we make by our projective desires, hopes, and actions, and so continually, as we pass through an ungraspable present, making and remaking a past. Time is neither our ally nor our enemy; it structures our existence, and to conceive our escape from it is to construct our lives, in time, in a certain way. To destroy time is to destroy ourselves; to destroy ourselves is to live in a certain temporality.

In *Tetrasomy Two,* a writer whom I know only by his pseudonym Oscar Rossiter invites us to contemplate a very special form of the return to a universal consciousness that is so pervasive in the genre. Here on Earth one man has been selected by the biological process to join other beings, selected by other kinds of biology, in a mental union that transcends the space-time matrix. *Tetrasomy Two* is a psychological drama that defers to genetics, and its historic past is reduced to that narrative past that belongs to novels situated in the present. When it reaches its conclusions, however, it escapes the demands of realistic plausibility altogether by annihilating time itself and in the same moment the solar system, whose sun provides the energy for the cataclysmic psychological change. When the future is mated to the past in the common consciousness of this novel, history—or at least human history—pays the price, as it always must in these images of the return to the preconscious origin.

At the beginning, where according to the necessities of the fiction of the future, there was that undifferentiated chaotic unity that the scriptures we know best describe as being subject to division—at the beginning is the womb of life, the promise of things to come, that is, separation. Those pods of *The Invasion of the Body Snatchers* are to the individual consciousness an alien source that the individual must leave behind and that, so the myths of mankind inform us, contain both good and evil. Few novels bring this ambiguous emotional evaluation to so persuasive a realization as does that model of hard science fiction *Rendezvous with Rama* by Arthur C. Clarke. The machinery, the technology, the hardware of the extrapolative sort of fiction achieves a kind of sublimity when the machine becomes a universe unto itself. Passing grandly through space, swinging by the sun in a graceful ricochet, the awesome space vehicle for a brief time astounds its human visitors. As an image in the constellation we are examining, where such futuristic perfections bear the value of a remote and unconscious past, Rama exhibits another kind of beauty. For the machine, we are delighted to learn, is nothing other than another pod, another unbroken egg—though it is threatened— incubating over aeons of time and parsecs of distance to give its creators another existence. When its human visitors finally grasp the cosmic dimensions of this scheme, they are contemplating again, as we do with undiminished interest in an inexhaustible set of possibilities, the journey up and down time, into the future and back, that promises us the loss of identity for the regaining of a new, and ordinarily higher, form of life. In *Rendezvous with Rama* this greater consciousness, which must, we recall, be transpersonal, is signified by the extraordinary singleness of intention, the remarkable unity of the machine, whose sole function is to preserve the life that created it. It is a symbiosis of machine and intelligence, life and nonlife, that Rama maintains, and if for a moment men walk within the egg, even if they endanger its fragile shell, it does continue on its way, toward that unimaginable future that beckons the genre, where the individuating and personal consciousness will be relieved of its burden of alienation. Prometheus is the god of this genre: the god who gave man forethinking. And he is also the image of that sinful intention that, to the gods, meant that man, in attempting to live beyond time, must be punished, condemned to time. It is this suffering consciousness that the genre expresses and for which it imagines, in various ways, a terrible and a beautiful relief. Human historicity, to attempt another and final formulation, when perfected in futurity, signifies not time but the lost, unknown, infinitely desirable, unrecapturable, Timeless beginning.

Brian Aldiss, with a fine invention, conceives of a simple solution to the endless paradoxes of time travel in *Cryptozoic*. Here the habitation of the past, at best shadowy, suddenly is recognized for what it truly is, a foreknowing of the future. Humanity has adopted the wrong perspective: what seems to unravel as a march of progress toward the future is the reel run backward. We are moving rather down the opposite slope toward what we took to be our beginning. The insight is, so far as science fiction is concerned, nearly definitive. The past looms before us in science fiction; the future is made, technically, historically, and psychologically, into a past, and the giant prolepsis may betray our lust for the end of time itself.

Notes

Incorporating Divinity: Platonic Science Fiction in the Middle Ages

1. Brian Aldiss, *Billion Year Spree: The True History of Science Fiction* (New York: Schocken, 1974), p. 8.

2. Darko Suvin, *Metamorphoses of Science Fiction* (New Haven: Yale University Press, 1979), p. viii.

3. For a discussion of Macrobius' theories and their revision by twelfth-century critics, see Peter Dronke, *Fabula: Explorations into the Uses of Myth in Medieval Platonism,* Mittellateinische Studien und Texte 9 (Leiden: Brill, 1974), pp 13–78.

4. "sciendum est tamen non in omnem disputationem philosophos admittere fabulosa . . .; sed his uti solent cum vel de anima vel de aeriis aetheriisve potestatibus vel de ceteris dis loquuntur" (*Commentarii in Somnium Scipionis* 1.2.13; ed. Jacob Willis [Leipzig: Teubner, 1963], p. 6. Trans. Dronke, p. 36).

5. "ceterum cum ad summum et principem omnium deum, qui apud Graecos τἀγαϑόν, qui πρῶτον αἴτιον nuncupatur, tractatus se audet attollere, vel ad mentem, quem Graeci νοῦν appellant, originales rerum species, quae ἰδέαι dictae sunt, continentem, ex summo natam et profectam deo: cum de his inquam loquuntur summo deo et mente, nihil fabulosum penitus attingunt" (*Comm. in Somn. Scip.* 1.2.14, pp. 6–7; trans. Dronke, p. 37 [material in brackets my translation]).

6. "quo nihil fas est de fabulis pervenire" (*Comm. in Somn. Scip.* 1.2.16, p. 7; trans. Dronke, p. 43).

7. *Myths of Plato* (1904; reprint ed., G. R. Levy, ed., Carbondale: Southern Illinois University Press, 1960), p. 171.

8. *The Republic of Plato,* trans. Francis Macdonald Cornford (1945; reprint ed., New York: Oxford University Press, 1968), p. 350.

9. *Republic* 10.616d; trans. Cornford, p. 353.

10. See Thomas S. Kuhn, *The Copernican Revolution: Planetary Astronomy in the Development of Western Thought* (Cambridge: Harvard University Press, 1957), pp. 55–59.

11. "artior quam solebat somnus" (*Somnium Scipionis 1.3; Willis, p. 156. Trans.*

H. A. Rice in World Masterpieces, *ed. Maynard Mack et al., 3d ed.* [New York: Norton, 1973] 1:566).

12. For Cicero this measure is the cosmic year, the time it takes the stars to return to a given original position. Macrobius' estimate for Cicero's "great year" is 15,000 solar years (*Comm. in Somn. Scip* 2.11.11; Willis, p. 129). See William Harris Stahl's translation of Macrobius, *Commentary on the Dream of Scipio,* Records of Civilization, Sources and Studies, No. 48 (New York: Columbia University Press, 1952), p. 221n.

13. "haec caelestia semper spectato, illa humana contemnito" (*Somn. Scip.* 6.1; Willis, p. 160. Trans. Rice, p. 570).

14. Edward Rosen, Introduction to *Kepler's Somnium: The Dream, or Posthumous Work on Lunar Astronomy,* trans. Edward Rosen (Madison: University of Wisconsin Press, 1967), p. xvii.

15. Kepler's notes to his *Dream* are longer than the *Dream* itself and offer an encyclopedic commentary on it similar to Macrobius' commentary on the *Dream of Scipio.*

16. "haec ita digerunt: primum sensum [vel locum] vestibulo quasi adsignant, secundum, puta, atrio, tum inpluvia circumeunt, nec cubiculis modo aut exedris, sed statuis etiam similibusque per ordinem committunt. hoc facto, cum est repetenda memoria, incipiunt ab initio loca haec recensere, et quod cuique crediderunt reposcunt, ut eorum imagine admonentur. ita, quamlibet multa sint, quorum meminisse oporteat, fiunt singula conexa quodam corio, nec errant coniunguntes prioribus consequentia solo ediscendi labore" (*Institutionis Oratoriae Libri XII* 11.2.20; ed. Ludwig Radermacher, with additions and corrections by Vinzenz Buchheit [Leipzig: Teubner, 1959], p. 318. Trans. Frances A. Yates, in *The Art of Memory* [Chicago: University of Chicago Press, 1966], p. 22).

17. ". . . ordinem esse, qui memoriae praecepta conferret. is uero in locis illustribus meditandus est, in quibus species rerum sententiarumque imagines collocandae sunt, ueluti nuptiarum uelatam flammeo nubentem aut homicidae gladium uel arma detineas, quas species locus tamquam depositas memoriae reddat. . . . si longiora fuerint, quae sunt ediscenda, diuisa per partes facilius inhaerescant; tum apponere notas rebus singulis oportebit in his, quae uolumus maxime retinere" (*De Nuptiis Philologiae et Mercurii* 5.538–39, in *Martianus Capella,* ed. Adolf Dick [Stuttgart: Teubner, 1969], p. 269). Trans. Yates, p. 51. For some reason Yates has not translated the phrase *sententiarumque imagines,* which I have rendered in brackets as "and the representations of ideas." Yates' translation of this passage differs markedly from that of Richard Johnson in *The Marriage of Philology and Mercury,* trans. William Harris Stahl and Richard Johnson with E. L. Budge, *Martianus Capella and the Seven Liberal Arts,* Records of Civilization, Sources and Studies, No. 84 (New York: Columbia University Press, 1977), 2:203–4 (all translations of Martianus taken from this volume). Johnson takes the phrase *in locis illustribus* to refer to "distinct topics" of rhetoric rather than the "well-lighted places" of the memory scheme. Such an interpretation would reduce Martianus' awareness of the art of memory to a minimum, or distort his understanding of it significantly. Since Martianus' chief source for the section on memory is Cicero's *De Oratore,* which makes it plain that the *loci* are physical places and not rhetorical topics (see Yates, pp. 17–18), I would suggest that Martianus is well aware of the imaginative construction of the memory building; however, since Cicero's account is also condensed and at times even cryp-

tic, Martianus' overall understanding of the art of memory may be somewhat askew.

18. "sed ipsi praesuli nunc draconis facies, nunc rictus leonis, nunc cristae cum aprinis dentibus uidebantur, totoque exitialis saeuiebat horrore, cui tamen potestas pro circi granditate maior ac praelata ceteris habebatur" (*De Nuptiis* 2.197, p. 75; trans. Johnson, p. 60).

19. *Allegory: The Theory of a Symbolic Mode* (Ithaca, N.Y.: Cornell University Press, 1964), p. 217.

20. For a good account of the topic see Glanville Downey, "Ekphrasis," *Reallexikon für Antike and Christentum; Sachwörterbuch zur Auseinandersetzung des Christentums mit der antchen Welt* (Stuttgart: Hiersemann, 1950–   ).

21. "et ecce globus quidam lucis aetheriae et concaua perspicui ignis aggestio, ut apparebat intra se quandam uirginem claudens, miti uertigine sensim inuolutus inlabitur. quo candore luminis propinquantis plures irradiati refulsere diui fatalesque maxime, quorum etiam habitus motusque et quicquid in his ignotum credebatur emicuit; tunc et ipsa extimi caeli contextio eiusdem lucis fulgoribus reuibrauit" (*De Nuptiis* 8.810, p. 428; trans. Stahl and Johnson, p. 317).

22. "quae ita ex omnibus compacta fuerat elementis, ut nihil abesset, quicquid ab omni creditur contineri natura. illic caelum omne, aer, freta diuersitasque telluris claustraque fuerant Tartarea; urbes etiam, completa cunctarumque species animantum tam in specie quam in genere numerandae. quae quidem sphaera imago quaedam uidebatur ideaque mundi. in hac quid cuncti, quid singuli nationum omnium populi cotidianis motibus agitarent, . . . speculo relucebat" (*De Nuptüs* 1.68, p. 32; trans. Johnson, p. 26).

23. "crocino circumlita exterius rutilabat ac dehinc perlucida inanitate albidoque humore, interiore tamen medio solidior apparebat" (*De Nuptiis* 2.140, p. 61; trans. Johnson, p. 48).

24. See *Fabula*, pp. 79–99, 154–66.

25. *The Quadrivium of Martianus Capella*, Volume 1 of *Martianus Capella and the Seven Liberal Arts*, Records of Civilization: Sources and Studies, No. 84 (New York: Columbia University Press, 1971), p. 89.

26. "fida recursio / interpresque meae mentis, ὁ νοῦς sacer" (*De Nuptiis* 1.92, p. 39; trans. Johnson, p. 31).

27. "salue uera deum facies uultusque paterne, / octo et sexcentis numeris, cui littera trina / conformat sacrum mentis cognomen et omen" (*De Nuptiis* 2.193, p. 74; trans. Johnson, p. 59).

28. "ac rationis apex diuumque hominisque sacer nus" (*De Nuptiis* 6.567, p. 285; trans. Stahl and Johnson, p. 215).

29. "ignoti uis celsa patris . . . / mentis fons" (*De Nuptiis* 2.185, p. 73; trans. Johnson, p. 58).

30. "tanti operis tantaeque rationis patrem deumque non ⟨ne⟩sciens ab ipsa etiam deorum notitia secessisse, quoniam extramundanas beatitudines eum transscendisse [*sic*] cognouerat empyrio quodam intellectualique mundo gaudentem" (*De Nuptiis* 2.202, p. 76; trans. Johnson, pp. 60–61).

31. *Quadrivium*, p. 87.

32. See *Quadrivium*, pp. 86–87. Relevant passages in *De Nuptiis*: 5, 8, 25, 29, 35, 92; 10–11, 20-22, 25, 26, 29, 191–93.

33. "celsior . . . Ioue" (*De Nuptiis* 6.567, p. 285; trans. Johnson, p. 215). See also *De Nuptiis* 567–574.

34. This might be construed as a misuse of the art of memory by Martianus (see note 17 above). Rather than being full of "well-lighted" places free to contain images, his universe is permanently full of fixed iconic forms. Thus his is an overdetermined hall of memory, all the slots of which are taken up by limited signifiers to which only certain concepts can be assigned. Martianus' cosmology is of course too complex to be subsumed entirely under any single interpretation, and I offer this analysis primarily to demonstrate how a knowledge of the ancient art of memory can help us understand the relation of the gods in the *Marriage*. Fannie LeMoine's *Martianus Capella: A Literary Re-evaluation*, Münchener Beiträge zur Mediävistik und Renaissance-Forschung 10 (Munich: Arbeo-Gesellschaft, 1972), amply shows the importance of harmony and number in the structure of the work, and the graphic descriptions of the gods have been compared to actual statues and tableaux of late antiquity (see LeMoine, p. 90 and nn.).

35. See Theodore Silverstein, "The Fabulous Cosmogony of Bernardus Silvestris," *Modern Philology* 46 (1948–49): 92–94.

36. Brian Stock, *Myth and Science in the Twelfth Century: A Study of Bernard Silvester* (Princeton: Princeton University Press, 1972), p. 19.

37. See ibid., pp. 20, 102–5.

38. Ibid., p. 20.

39. "Natura ad Noym, id est Dei providentiam, de primae materiae, id est hyles, confusione querimoniam quasi cum lacrimis agit et ut mundus pulcrius expoliatur petit. Noys igitur eius mota precibus petitioni libenter annuit et ita quatuor elementa ab invicem seiungit. Novem ierarchias angelorum in caelo ponit. stellas in firmamento figit. signa disponit. sub signis orbes septem planetarum currere facit. quatuor ventos cardinales sibi invicem opponit. Sequitur genesis animantium et terrae situs medius. Postea montes famosi describuntur. sequitur proprietas animalium. deinde famosi fluvii. sequitur proprietas arborum. postea species odoratae describuntur. deinde genera leguminum. proprietas aristarum. deinde virtus herbarum. postea genera natatilium. sequitur genus avium. postea unde vita animantibus sit disseritur. Itaque in primo libro ornatus elementorum describitur" (*Cosmographia*, Breviarium, in *Bernardi Silvestris De Mundi Universitate Libri Duo sive Megacosmus et Microcosmus*, ed. Carl Sigmund Barach and Johann Wrobel [1876; reprint ed. Frankfurt am Main: Minerva, 1964], pp. 5–6; trans. Winthrop Wetherbee, *The "Cosmographia" of Bernardus Silvestris*, Records of Civilization: Sources and Studies, No. 89 [New York: Columbia University Press, 1973], pp. 65–66).

40. "contractaque carica rugis, / fructus Adae ficus" (*Cos.* 1.3.287–88, p. 23; trans. Wetherbee, p. 82); "bubo, solis quam caecat amabile lumen" (*Cos.* 1.3.477, p. 29; trans. Wetherbee, p. 86); "Commendat Ligerim darsus" (*Cos.* 1.3.following 438. The line does not appear in Barach and Wrobel's edition; Wetherbee takes the reading from MS Oxford Bodleian Laud Misc. 585 [see Wetherbee, p. 64]. Trans. Wetherbee, p. 85).

41. "Ut res dissimiles uniat unus amor" (*Cos.* 2.8.28, p. 51; trans. Wetherbee, p. 109).

42. Peter Dronke, "L'amor che move il sole e l'altre stelle," *Studi Medievali*, 3d ser. 6, Fasc. 1 (1965): 413.

43. "Sicut enim divinae semper voluntatis est praegnans, sic exemplis aeternarum quas gestat imaginum noys endelechiam, endelechia naturam, natura imarmenem quid mundo debeat informavit" (*Cos.* 1.4.120–24, p. 32; trans. Wetherbee, p. 90).

44. "Integumentum est genus demostrationis sub fabulosa narratione veritatis involvens intellectum, unde etiam dicitur involucrum." This definition appears in the *accessus* to the commentary on the first six books of the *Aeneid* attributed to Bernardus Silvestris. *Commentum Quod Dicitur Bernardi Silvestris super Sex Libros Eneidos Virgilii,* ed. Julian Ward Jones and Elizabeth Frances Jones (Lincoln: University of Nebraska Press, 1977), p. 3.

45. "Integumentum uero est oratio sub fabulosa narratione uerum claudens intellectum" (MS Cambridge University Library Mm.I.18, f. Irb; cited in Stock, p. 38).

46. "sicut vulgaribus hominum sensibus intellectum sui vario rerum tegmine operimentoque subtraxit, ita a prudentibus arcana sua voluit per fabulosa tractari" (*Comm. in Somn. Scip.* 1.2.17, p. 7; my translation).

47. See Stock, pp. 88–89.

48. "Dei ratio profundius exquisita, quam utique de se alteram se usia prima genuit. . . .scientia et divinae voluntatis arbitraria ad dispositionem rerum" (*Cos.* 1.2.6–10, p. 9; trans. Wetherbee, p. 69).

49. "mens aeterna, in qua sensus ille profundissimus, in qua rerum genitor extortorque omnium intellectus" (*Cos.* 2.11.26–28, p. 57; trans. Wetherbee, p. 115).

50. See note 5 above.

51. See note 5 above.

52. "summi et superessentialis Dei sacrarium" (*Cos.* 2.5.10, p. 40; trans. Wetherbee, p. 98).

53. "Ex sedibus quidem . . . splendor emicat radiatus, non utique perfunctorius, sed infinibilis et aeternus. Ea igitur lux inaccessibilis intendentis reverberat oculos, aciem praeconfundit, ut quia lumen se defendit a lumine, splendorem ex se videas caliginem peperisse" (*Cos.* 2.5.23–29, p. 41; trans. Wetherbee, p. 99). Stock interprets *Tugaton* not as God, but as his palace or residence (p. 172); I follow Wetherbee, who equates the name with Macrobius's *tagathon* and the supreme deity himself.

54. Especially in his letters and the *Mystical Theology.* On Pseudo-Dionysius (probably a Syrian monk of the sixth century who, in an attempt to lend his writings authenticity, ascribed them to the Dionysius converted by St. Paul on the Areopagus [Acts 17:34]), see I. P. Sheldon-Williams, "The Pseudo-Dionysius," in *The Cambridge History of Later Greek and Early Medieval Philosophy,* ed. A. H. Armstrong (Cambridge: At the University Press, 1967), pp. 457–72.

Dialogues Concerning Human Understanding: Empirical Views of God from Locke to Lem

1. Stanislaw Lem, *Solaris,* trans. Joanna Kilmartin and Steve Cox (New York: Berkley Medallion, 1971), p. 81.

2. Ibid., p. 132.

3. Ibid., p. 178.

4. Ibid., p. 180.

5. Stanislaw Lem, *The Investigation,* trans. Adele Milch (New York: Avon, 1976), p. 111.

6. John Locke, *An Essay Concerning Humane Understanding,* ed. and annotated by Alexander Campbell Fraser (1894; reprint ed., New York: Dover, 1959) 2:306–7.

7. *Dialogues Concerning Natural Religion,* ed. and intro. Henry D. Aiken (New York: Hafner, 1948), pp. 22, 23.

8. Ibid., p. 94.

9. Heinz Politzer, *Franz Kafka: Parable and Paradox* (Ithaca, N. Y.: Cornell, University Press, 1966), p. 371.

10. To mention only two, Darko Suvin, Afterword to Lem, *Solaris,* p. 222; and Jerzy Jarzebski, "Stanislaw Lem, Rationalist and Visionary," in *Science Fiction Studies: Second Series,* ed. R. D. Mullen and Darko Suvin (Boston: Gregg Press, 1978), p. 226.

11. Stainislaw Lem, *Memoirs Found in a Bathtub,* trans. Michael Kandel and Christine Rose (New York: Seabury, 1973), p. 186.

12. A brief response to Suvin's credulity appears in David Ketterer, "*Solaris* and the Illegitimate Suns of Science Fiction," *Extrapolation* 14 (December 1972):84.

13. Lem, *Solaris,* p. 206.

14. Stanislaw Lem, *The Star Diaries,* trans. Michael Kandel (New York: Avon, 1977), p. 268.

15. Ibid., p. 230.

16. Ibid., pp. 224–25.

17. Lem, *Solaris,* p. 203.

18. Ibid., p. 210.

19. Ibid., p. 211.

Aliens and Knowability: A Scientist's Perspective

1. Stanislaw Lem, *Solaris,* trans. Joanna Kilmartin and Steve Cox (New York: Berkley Medallion, 1971), p. 222.

2. Ibid., p. 220.

Visionary States and the Search for Transcendence in Science Fiction

1. Two examples are Robert Scholes and Eric S. Rabkin, *Science Fiction: History, Science, Vision* (New York: Oxford University Press, 1977), pp. 165–69, 207–26; and *The Visual Encyclopedia of Science Fiction,* ed. Brian Ash (New York: Harmony Books, 1977), pp. 223–36.

2. For the classic description of this experience see Evelyn Underhill, *Mysticism* (New York: Dutton, 1910).

3. Ian Watson, *The Embedding* (New York: Scribner's, 1973), p. 157.

4. Ibid., p. 158.

5. Ibid.

6. Ibid., p. 108.

7. Philip K. Dick, *The Three Stigmata of Palmer Eldritch* (Garden City, N.Y.: Doubleday, 1965), p. 276.

8. Philip K. Dick, "Man, Android, and Machine," in *Science Fiction at Large,* ed. Peter Nicholls (New York: Harper and Row, 1976), p. 204.

9. Dick, *The Three Stigmata,* p. 270.

10. Philip K. Dick, "Faith of Our Fathers," in *Dangerous Visions,* ed. Harlan Ellison (1967; reprint ed., New York: New American Library, 1975), p. 167.

11. The reference is to Dick, "Man, Android, and Machine," pp. 208–10.

12. Robert Silverberg, *A Time of Changes* (New York: New American Library, 1971), p. 134.

13. Ibid., p. 201.

14. Ibid., pp. 219–20.

15. Robert Silverberg, *Downward to the Earth* (New York: New American Library, 1971), p. 173.

16. Ibid., pp. 174–75.

17. Ibid., p. 176.

Fairy Tales and Science Fiction

1. Jakob Grimm and Wilhelm Grimm, "The Frog Prince," in *Household Stories of the Brothers Grimm*, trans. Lucy Crane. (New York: Dover, 1963 [1886]), p. 32.

2. Nathaniel Hawthorne, "Earth's Holocaust," in *Science Fiction: The Future* ed. Dick Allen (New York: Harcourt Brace Jovanovich, 1971 [1844]), p. 49.

3. Lewis Carroll, *Through the Looking-Glass*, in *The Annotated Alice*, ed. Martin Gardner (New York: World Publishing, 1971 [1872]), p. 247.

4. Hawthorne, pp. 51–52.

5. Quoted by Jeremy Bernstein, "Out of the Ego Chamber," *New Yorker*, 9 August 1969, p. 52.

6. Jakob Grimm and Wilhelm Grimm, "The Three Spinsters," in *Household Stories of the Brothers Grimm*, trans. Lucy Crane (New York: Dover, 1963 [1886]), p. 84.

7. Grimm and Grimm, "The Frog Prince," p. 35.

8. Mary Shelley, *Frankenstein* (New York: Collier, 1971 [1818]), p. 97.

9. Isaac Asimov, "Evidence," in *I, Robot* (Greenwich, Conn.: Fawcett, 1970 [1946])., p. 152.

10. Max Lüthi, *Once Upon a Time: On the Nature of Fairy Tales*, trans. Lee Chadeayne and Pal Gottwald (New York: Frederick Ungar, 1970), p. 45.

11. Ray Bradbury, "Ylla," *The Martian Chronicles*, (New York: Bantam, 1970 [1950]), p. 2.

12. Lüthi, p. 51.

13. Ibid., p. 77.

14. James Gunn, "Science Fiction and the Mainstream," in *Science Fiction: Today and Tomorrow*, ed. Reginald Bretnor, (Baltimore: Penguin, 1974), p. 190.

15. Hugo Gernsback and F. Orlin Tremaine, quoted in Paul A. Carter, *The Creation of Tomorrow: Fifty Years of Magazine Science Fiction* (New York: Columbia University Press, 1977), pp. 4, 16.

16. Robert A. Heinlein, *The Puppet Masters* (New York: Signet, 1951), p. 175.

17. Agatha Christie, *The A.B.C. Murders* (New York: Pocket Books, 1973 [1936]), p. 65.

18. Bruno Bettelheim, *The Uses of Enchantment* (New York: Knopf, 1976), pp. 45–53.

19. Carter, p. 173.

20. Lloyd Biggle, Jr., *Monument* (New York: Bantam, 1978 [1974]), pp. 5, 113.

21. Spider Robinson, *Callahan's Crosstime Saloon* (New York: Ace, 1977), p. 102.

22. Hugo Gernsback, *Ralph 124C 41+* (New York: Frederick Fell, 1950 [1925]), p. 25.

23. Ibid., p. 205.

24. Arthur C. Clarke, *The Lion of Comarre*, in *The Lion of Comarre & Against the Fall of Night* (New York: Harcourt, Brace & World, 1968 [1949]), p. 19.

25. Ibid., p. 46.

26. Arthur C. Clarke, *The City and the Stars* (New York: Harbrace, 1969 [1956], p. 3.

27. Arthur C. Clarke, *Against the Fall of Night*, in *The Lion of Comarre & Against the Fall of Night* (New York: Harcourt, Brace & World, 1968 [1953]), p. 107.

28. Clarke, *The City and the Stars*, p. 17.

29. Gregory Benford, *In the Ocean of Night* (New York: Dell, 1978 [1977]), p. 329.

30. Stanislaw Lem, *The Cyberiad*, trans. Michael Kandel (New York: Avon, 1976 [1967]), p. 236.

Science Fiction as Truncated Epic

1. Northrop Frye, *Anatomy of Criticism* (Princeton: Princeton University Press, 1957), p. 49.

2. Darko Suvin, "On the Poetics of the Science Fiction Genre," in *Science Fiction: A Collection of Critical Essays*, ed. Mark Rose (Englewood Cliffs, N.J.: Prentice-Hall, 1976), pp. 57–71.

3. Pound, quoted in Paul Merchant, *The Epic* (London: Methuen, 1971), p. 1.

4. Gillian Beer, *The Romance* (London: Methuen, 1970), p. 8.

5. Robert Louis Stevenson, *Memories and Portraits* (London: Heinemann, 1924), p. 122.

6. For myth criticism, see Frye; for examples of literary structuralism, see Vladimir Propp, *Morphology of the Folktale*, trans. Lawrence Scott (Bloomington: Indiana University Press, 1958), (1928), and, in an American context, John G. Cawelti, *Adventure, Mystery, and Romance* (Chicago: University of Chicago Press, 1976).

7. See Robert H. Canary, "Science Fiction as Fictive History," *Extrapolation* 16 (December 1974): 81–95, an article I have found particularly useful.

8. Robert A. Heinlein, "Science Fiction: Its Nature, Faults and Virtues," in *The Science Fiction Novel: Imagination and Social Criticism*, ed. Basil Davenport (Chicago: Advent, 1969), p. 22.

9. H. G. Wells, "Fiction about the Future," typescript, Wells Collection, University of Illinois Library. (This unpublished talk was broadcast over Australian radio on 29 December 1938.)

10. Georg Lukács, *The Theory of the Novel*, trans. Anna Bostock (London: Merlin Press, 1971), pp. 46, 78–81.

11. Lukács, *The Historical Novel*, trans. Hannah and Stanley Mitchell (London: Merlin Press, 1969), p. 63.

12. Ibid., p. 189.

13. See Mark R. Hillegas, "Second Thoughts on the Course in Science Fiction." in *Science Fiction: The Academic Awakening*, ed. Willis E. McNelly, supplement to *CEA Critic* 37 (November 1974): 17.

14. H. G. Wells, *The Time Machine* (London: Heinemann, 1949), p. 90.

15. See George Locke, "Wells in Three Volumes?" *Science-Fiction Studies* 3 (November 1976): 282–86.

16. Wells, pp. 30–32.

17. Ibid., pp. 143–44.

18. See Charles Elkins, "Science Fiction Versus Futurology," *Science-Fiction Studies* 6 (March 1979): 20–31.

19. Isaac Asimov, quoted in John Huntington, "Science Fiction and the Future," in *Science Fiction: A Collection of Critical Essays,* ed. Mark Rose (Englewood Cliffs, N.J.: Prentice-Hall, 1976), p. 165.

20. J. B. S. Haldane, *Possible Worlds and Other Essays* (London: Chatto and Windus, 1927), p. 292.

21. Ibid., p. 295.

22. H. G. Wells, *Things to Come* (New York: Macmillan, 1935), pp. 154–55.

23. Canary, p. 85.

24. See R. D. Mullen, "Blish, Van Vogt, and the Uses of Spengler," *Riverside Quarterly* 3 (August 1968): 172–86.

25. J. D. Bernal, *The World, the Flesh and the Devil* (London: Cape Editions, 1971), p. 46.

26. Heinlein, *Orphans of the Sky* (New York: Berkley Medallion, 1970), pp. 127–28.

27. *The Best Short Stories of J. G. Ballard* (New York: Holt, Rinehart and Winston, 1978), p. 159.

28. Stanislaw Lem, *Solaris,* trans. Joanna Kilmartin and Steve Cox (London: Arrow Books, 1973), p. 204.

29. For further discussion of the literature of scientific anticipation, and a brief bibliography, see Patrick Parrinder, "Science Fiction and the Scientific World-View," in *Science Fiction: A Critical Guide,* ed. Patrick Parrinder (London and New York: Longman, 1979), pp. 67–88.

Science Fiction and the Gothic

1. Brian Aldiss, *Billion Year Spree: The True History of Science Fiction* (Garden City, N.Y.: Doubleday, 1973), p. 18.

2. Leslie Fiedler, *Love and Death in the American Novel,* 2d ed. (New York: Stein and Day, 1966), p. 500.

3. See Wolfgang Kayser, *The Grotesque in Art and Literature,* trans. Ulrich Weisstein (1963; reprint ed., New York: McGraw-Hill, 1966), pp. 179–89.

4. Matthew G. Lewis, *The Monk* (New York: Grove Press, 1952), p. 385.

5. Philip R. Dick, *Ubik* (New York: Bantam, 1977), p. 152.

6. My use of this term is based on Angus Fletcher's analysis and application of the concept of daemonic agency in the first chapter of *Allegory: The Theory of a Symbolic Mode* (Ithaca, N.Y.: Cornell University Press, 1964).

7. Ibid.

8. Olaf Stapledon, *Last and First Men* (1931; reprint ed., New York: Dover, 1968), p. 10.

9. Tzvetan Todorov, *The Fantastic: A Structural Approach to a Literary Genre,* trans. Richard Howard (Cleveland: Case Western Reserve University Press, 1973), p. 113.

10. Cf. Ursula K. Le Guin on *The Left Hand of Darkness:* "Yes, indeed the people in it are androgynous, but that doesn't mean that I'm predicting that in a millennium or so we will all be androgynous, or announcing that I think we damned well ought to

be androgynous. I'm merely observing, in the peculiar, devious, and thought-experimental manner proper to science fiction, that if you look at us at certain odd times of day in certain weathers, we already are. I am not predicting or prescribing. I am describing. I am describing certain aspects of psychological reality in the novelist's way, inventing elaborately circumstantial lies" (Introduction to *The Left Hand of Darkness* [New York: Ace Books, 1976], p. v).

11. Darko Suvin, "On the Poetics of the Science Fiction Genre," *College English* 34 (1972), reprinted in *Science Fiction: A Collection of Critical Essays,* ed. Mark Rose (Englewood Cliffs, N.J.: Prentice-Hall, 1976), p. 59.

Robert Scholes speaks of this facet of science fiction as "fabulation": "Fabulation, then, is fiction that offers us a world clearly and radically discontinuous from the one we know, yet returns to confront that known world in some cognitive way" (*Structural Fabulation: An Essay on Fiction of the Future* [Notre Dame, Ind.: University of Notre Dame Press, 1976], p. 29).

Philip Dick's *Man in the High Castle* and the Nature of Science-Fictional Worlds

1. The predominance of these themes has been remarked by other critics. See, for example, almost any of the essays from the issue of *Science-Fiction Studies* devoted to Dick, reprinted in *Science-Fiction Studies: Selected Essays,* ed. R. D. Mullen and Darko Suvin (Boston: Gregg Press, 1976), pp. 159–232.

2. Philip K. Dick, *The Man in the High Castle* (1962; reprint ed., New York: Berkley Medallion, 1974), p. 18.

3. Ibid., p. 251.

4. Ibid.

5. I borrow the phrase from John Barth's *Chimera.*

6. Dick, p. 43.

7. Ibid., p. 44.

8. Carlo Pagetti, "Dick and Meta-Science Fiction," trans. Angela Minchella and D. Suvin, in *Science Fiction Studies: Selected Essays,* ed. R. D. Mullen and Darko Suvin (Boston: Gregg Press, 1976), p. 182.

9. Dick, p. 95.

10. Ibid., p. 239.

11. What happens, most interestingly, when Tagomi seeks out the "truth" of Frink's piece is that he is transported from one world to another, which just happens to correspond to San Francisco as it "really" was in 1962. The artwork takes Tagomi to the world of the Real! Dick, pp. 217–25.

12. Dick, p. 230.

13. One might cite here, as representative examples of this sort of analysis, Wayne Booth, *The Rhetoric of Fiction* (1961; reprint ed., Chicago: University of Chicago Press, 1975); Franz Stanzel, *Narrative Situations in the Novel,* trans. James P. Pusack (Bloomington: Indiana University Press, 1971); and Lubomir Dolezel, "The Typology of the Narrator: Point of View in Fiction," in *To Honor Roman Jacobson: Essays on the Occasion of His 70th Birthday,* no editor (Paris: Mouton, 1967), 1:541–53. The texts are listed according to increasing rigor in critical methodology.

14. For excerpts from Reeve's argument, see *Novelists on the Novel,* ed. Miriam Allott (New York: Columbia University Press, 1959), pp. 45, 47, 86–87.

15. Lubomir Dolezel, "Narrative Modalities," *Journal of Literary Semantics* 5 (April 1976): 9–10.

16. As a matter of fact, there has been a great deal of interesting and fruitful work done of late using the component of plot as the armature for a "grammar of stories." See, for example, Gerald Prince, *A Grammar of Stories* (The Hague: Mouton, 1973); Lubomir Dolezel, "Narrative Semantics," *PTL* 1 (January 1976): 129–52, and idem, "Narrative Modalities"; Edward Kahn, "Finite-State Modals of Plot Complexity," *Poetics* 9 (1973): 5–20. A discussion aimed at a more rigorous definition of plot and an exploration of its effect can be found in Kieran Egan, "What Is Plot?" *New Literary History* 9 (Spring 1978): 455–73. See also Jurij Lotman, *The Structure of the Artistic Text*, trans. Ronald Vroon (Ann Arbor: University of Michigan Press, 1977), pp. 231–44.

17. Reprinted in *Science Fiction: The Other Side of Realism*, ed. Thomas D. Clareson (Bowling Green, O.: Bowling Green University Popular Press, 1971), pp. 130–45.

18. Ursula Le Guin, *The Left Hand of Darkness* (1969; reprint ed., New York: Ace, 1976), no page; Darko Suvin, "On the Poetics of the Science Fiction Genre," in *Science Fiction: A Collection of Critical Essays*, ed. Mark Rose (Englewood Cliffs, N.J.: Prentice-Hall, 1976), pp. 57–71; Robert Scholes, *Structural Fabulation: An Essay on Fiction of the Future* (Notre Dame, Ind.: University of Notre Dame Press, 1975), pp. 27–45.

19. John Huntington, "Science Fiction and the Future," in *Science Fiction: A Collection of Critical Essays*, ed. Mark Rose (Englewood Cliffs, N.J.: Prentice-Hall, 1976), pp. 156–66.

20. See Lee T. Lemon and Marion J. Reis, eds., *Russian Formalist Criticism: Four Essays* (Lincoln: University of Nebraska Press, 1965).

21. Jonathan Culler, *Structuralist Poetics* (Ithaca, N.Y.: Cornell University Press, 1975), pp. 141–45.

22. For somewhat different views on the nature of the fantastic in literature and the genre of fantasy see Tzvetan Todorov, *The Fantastic: A Structural Approach to Literary Genre*, trans. Richard Howard (Cleveland, O.: Case Western Reserve University Press, 1973); and Eric S. Rabkin, *The Fantastic in Literature* (Princeton, N.J.: Princeton University Press, 1976).

23. See, for example, L. David Allen's "Categories of Science Fiction," in his *Science Fiction: Reader's Guide* (Lincoln, Neb.: Centennial Press, 1973), pp. 5–14.

The Past of Science Fiction

1. Kingsley Amis, *New Maps of Hell* (New York: Harcourt, Brace, 1960), p. 18.

2. Samuel R. Delany, *Triton* (New York: Bantam, 1976), p.

3. Jonathan Culler, *Structuralist Poetics: Structuralism, Linguistics, and the Study of Literature* (Ithaca, N.Y.: Cornell University Press, 1976), p. 136.

4. Eric Rabkin, *The Fantastic in Literature* (Princeton: Princeton University Press, 1976), pp. 8–13.

5. Tzvetan Todorov, *The Fantastic: A Structural Approach to a Literary Genre*, trans. Richard Howard (Ithaca, N.Y.: Cornell University Press, 1975).

6. See Northrop Frye, *Anatomy of Criticism* (Princeton: Princeton University Press, 1957), pp. 141–50.

7. Paul Ricoeur, *Symbolism of Evil,* trans. Emerson Buchanan (New York: Beacon Press, 1969), pp. 161–71.

8. Frank Kermode, *Sense of an Ending: Studies in the Theory of Fiction* (Oxford: Oxford University Press, 1966), p. 59.

Biographical Notes

Gregory Benford is Professor of Physics at the University of California, Irvine, and is well known as a science fiction writer.

George Guffey, who has degrees in science and literature, is Professor of English at the University of California, Los Angeles, and has published on seventeenth- and eighteenth-century English literature.

Thomas A. Hanzo is Professor of English and Chairman of the Department of English at the University of California, Davis, and has published on seventeenth-century and modern literature.

Robert Hunt holds the Ph.D. degree in English from the University of California, Los Angeles, and is presently an editor at Glencoe Publishing.

Thomas H. Keeling is Lecturer in English at the University of California, Los Angeles, and is completing a book on gothic fiction.

Kent T. Kraft is Assistant Professor of Comparative Literature at the University of Georgia and specializes in medieval literature and the history of science.

Harry Levin is Irving Babbitt Professor of Comparative Literature at Harvard University.

Carl D. Malmgren teaches English at the University of Oregon and is currently working on a theory of narrative.

Patrick Parrinder is Reader in English at the University of Reading, England, and has published on H. G. Wells and science fiction.

Stephen W. Potts teaches in the writing program at San Diego State University and is also a science fiction writer.

Eric S. Rabkin is Professor of English at the University of Michigan and has published on literary and narrative theory as well as on science fiction.

Mark Rose is Professor of English at the University of California, Santa Barbara, and has published on Shakespeare and Renaissance literature.

George Slusser is Lecturer in Comparative Literature and Curator of the Eaton Collection at the University of California, Riverside, and has published on European Romanticism as well as on science fiction, fantasy, and science and literature.

Index